ISBN 978-0-266-22398-6
PIBN 10242027

BELL'S CATHEDRAL SERIES

BATH ABBEY

MALMESBURY ABBEY

ST. LAURENCE, BRADFORD-ON-AVON

BATH ABBEY, THE NAVE, LOOKING WEST.

THE ABBEY CHURCHES OF
BATH & MALMESBURY
AND THE CHURCH OF SAINT LAURENCE, BRADFORD-ON-AVON

BY
THE REV. T. PERKINS, M.A.
RECTOR OF TURNWORTH, DORSET

WITH FORTY-NINE   ILLUSTRATIONS

ARMS OF BATH ABBEY

LONDON   GEORGE   BELL   &   SONS   1901

AUTHOR'S PREFACE

THE present volume is the outcome of personal examination of the three buildings described, supplemented by information gathered from various sources, among them papers by Professor Freeman, Canon Jones, Canon Jackson, and others, published in the Transactions of the Wilts Archæological and Natural History Society.

My best thanks are due to Canon Quirk, D.D., Rector of Bath, and to the Rev. G. W. Tucker, M.A., Vicar of Malmesbury, for facilities readily granted to me to photograph their respective churches; to Messrs. Basey and Player, vergers, for much interesting information; to Mr. Bilson, and the Secretary of the Royal Institute of British Architects, for permission to use the plan reproduced on p. 92; to Mr. Brakspear, the architect who has charge of the restoration work at Malmesbury, for sending measurements and information respecting that church; and, lastly, to an amateur, who desires to remain anonymous, for the use of the photographs reproduced on pp. 32, 80. These were taken before the restoration was begun, from points of view not now available on account of scaffolding erected against the building, and so are of special interest.

TURNWORTH, BLANDFORD,
April, 1901.

CONTENTS

BATH ABBEY CHURCH.

MALMESBURY ABBEY CHURCH.

b

CONTENTS.

LIST OF ILLUSTRATIONS

B

BATH ABBEY, THE EAST END.

THE ABBEY CHURCH OF
ST. PETER, BATH.

CHAPTER I.

HISTORY OF THE BUILDING.

THE chief interest of Bath Abbey, as we see it to-day, is that the whole of the building is of so late a date that we may regard it as the last complete ecclesiastical building erected before the dissolution of the monasteries. Henry VII.'s Chapel at Westminster, which, though attached to the abbey, may in a certain sense be considered complete in itself, is its only contemporary rival. Nothing of importance in Gothic art was done in England after the Reformation; and as Bath Abbey Church was not actually finished, though it was nearing completion, when it was surrendered to Henry VIII. in 1539, we may consider it the last expression of Gothic, and, comparing it with the work of preceding centuries, we shall come to the conclusion that Gothic, even had there been no Reformation to put an end to church building, was rapidly approaching the hour of its death.

But though in Bath Abbey, as it stands to-day, we see nothing, save a few fragments of the foundations, of earlier date than the sixteenth century, yet a Christian church existed here from very early times; and the history of Bath goes back to a still earlier date—for the natural hot springs and the genial climate of the Avon Valley attracted the Roman conquerors to the spot. Here they were able to enjoy some of the chief luxuries they had been accustomed to in their own far-off southern land; here they built a splendid temple to the honour of Sul Minerva, and called the city Aquæ Sulis; here, too, they constructed extensive baths, which have been excavated in recent times, and still more recently have been spoilt by the building of imitation Roman colonnades round them. The Temple of Sul Minerva has entirely vanished save for a few sculptured stones that are preserved in the museum at Bath In the year 577 the city was captured by the West Saxons, and, like Malmesbury, at different times was under the rule of West Saxon and Mercian kings respectively. It is said, but on doubtful authority, that in the year 676 the Hwiccian King Osric founded a nunnery here, and it is certain that Offa, the Mercian king, about the year 775 founded a college of secular canons at Bath. In the tenth century these canons shared the fate of many other bodies of secular clergy, and were expelled by Dunstan, and their place taken by monks. To Bath in the year 973 King Edgar came with great pomp, and on the day of the Feast of Pentecost was crowned in the abbey church. To commemorate this event it was customary, up to so late a date as Leland's time, to elect on Whitsunday, from among the citizens, one who bore the title of " King of Bath."

At the time of the Norman Conquest, Ælfsige was abbot, and he, though an Englishman, managed to keep his office throughout the reign of William I. and until his death, which occurred in the reign of William II.

At this time John de Villula, a Frenchman from Tours, was Bishop of Somerset, having his bishop-stool at the Church of St. Andrew, at Wells. But, dissatisfied with his bishopric, he persuaded William Rufus to grant him the abbey church at Bath; this was done by charter in 1088, and the grant was confirmed by two charters of Henry I., dated respectively 1100 and 1111. In the second we find this passage : " Batha ubi frater meus Willielmus et ego constituimus et confirmavimus sedem episcopatûs totius Summersetæ, quæ olim erat apud villam quæ dicitur Wella." John also obtained from William a grant of the site and ruins of the town of Bath, which had recently been destroyed by fire. The Abbey of Bath thus was merged in the bishopric. It had no longer an abbot of its own; the bishop was nominally its abbot; the prior and monks formed the bishop's chapter. Bishop John ruled the monks—who were no doubt for the most part Englishmen—very sternly ; he was a learned man himself, and he despised the monks as ignorant barbarians. "Aliquantum dure in monachos agebat," says William of Malmesbury, "quod essent hebetes et ejus æstimatione barbari." Having gained possession of Bath, he forthwith set to work to rebuild the church dedicated to St. Peter, and on its completion he transferred to it the bishop's seat from the Church of St. Andrew, at Wells. So, to once more quote the words of William, "Cessit enim Andreas Simoni fratri, frater major minori." The see was now called the Bishopric of Bath. John died in 1122, and was succeeded by Godfrey of Lorraine, who held the bishopric till his death in 1135.

The next bishop was Robert, by descent a Fleming, but English born. He had been a monk at Lewes ; and when Henry, King Stephen's brother, who had been Abbot of Glastonbury, became Bishop of Worcester, he sent Robert to act as his deputy at Glastonbury, for Henry did not resign the lucrative post of abbot of the wealthiest abbey in the West. On Godfrey's death he became Bishop of Bath.

Robert set himself to get his diocese out of the state of confusion into which John of Tours had plunged it by transferring his episcopal seat from Wells to Bath. It would seem that an arrangement was made by which, though Bath was to have the precedence, yet the Bishop of Somerset was to have a throne at both the churches—St. Andrew, at Wells, and St. Peter, at Bath ; and the bishop was to be chosen jointly by the monks of Bath and the canons of Wells.

During Bishop Robert's time the church at Bath again suffered from its old enemy, fire, and the church built by John of Tours was so much damaged that it had to be largely rebuilt by Robert. Under him the cathedral church at Bath reached its greatest perfection. His successors seem to have looked with greater favour on Wells, and to have made that more and more their chief place of residence, so that Bath was neglected.

Roger (1244–1247) may, according to Professor Freeman, be considered the last Bath bishop. When the great Jocelin died, the monks of Bath, without consulting the Canons of Wells, obtained a *congé d'élire* of Henry III. ; elected Roger, he was confirmed in his bishopric by Pope

Innocent IV., who paid no heed to the protest of the Canons of Wells. The pope, however, made it a condition that his own nephew should succeed to the Precentorship of Salisbury vacated by Roger, and then, having thus obtained perferment for his kinsman, agreed that for the future the Canons of Wells should take part in the election. Roger's episcopate was a short one. On his death he was buried at Bath—the last of the pre-Reformation Bishops of Bath and Wells to choose St. Peter's as his last resting-place.

But though the bishops neglected Bath, they still were abbots of the monastery, and drew their share of the abbey revenues. Thus the monastery was much impoverished, and suffered as property usually does when the rents are drawn by an absentee, and spent elsewhere. Hence it came to pass that at the end of the fifteenth century the church was in a ruinous condition, even to its foundations.

It chanced that in the year 1495, Oliver King, previously Bishop of Exeter, was translated to the See of Bath and Wells, and soon after his appointment it happened that he was at Bath. It may be that the sad state of neglect in which he found the church made a vivid impression on his mind, but, whether this were so or not, he fell asleep, and while he slept he dreamed, and, behold, a ladder, near the foot of which grew an olive-tree, set up on the earth, and the top of it reached to heaven, and, behold, the angels of God ascending and descending on it, and, behold, the Lord stood above it and said, " Let an Olive establish the crown and a King restore the church." And he waked up out of his sleep and said unto himself, " Surely the Lord spake unto me, and as He has charged me so will I do." That vision of Bishop Oliver King may still be seen carved on the west front of the church. On each of the turrets at the two west corners of the nave are ladders set up, with angels ascending and descending, and on the west face on each of the corner buttresses is carved an olive issuing from a crown.

About 1500, the ruins having been cleared away, Bishop King set about the work of rebuilding ; but, having calculated the cost, he did not feel himself justified in making the new church of the same size as the old one ; in fact, the new church, including the choir and aisles, only occupies the site of the nave of the church built by Bishop John. Bishop King

PRIOR BIRDE'S CHANTRY.

did not live long enough to see the new work brought to completion; neither the south nor west part were roofed in, nor had the walls even been raised to their full height when he died in 1503.

The prior at this time was one William Birde, whose rebus— a W and a Bird—may be seen in many parts of the building. He, after Bishop King's death, went on with the work till his death in 1525. The choir must have been nearly, if not entirely, finished, as the prior built himself a chantry chapel between the choir and its south aisle.

Prior Holloway went on with the work, but before the building had been completed the monastery and the church were seized by the king's commissioners; the lead, glass, and bells, sold, after the church had been offered to the city for a small sum —500 marks. More niggardly, or caring less about the church than the inhabitants of many other places, who paid the sum requisite to purchase the church as a place of worship for the town, the citizens of Bath refused the offer, and thus everything that could be converted into money was stripped from the building.

Finally, the abbey buildings passed into the hands of one Matthew Colthurst, whose son in 1560 gave to the city the "carcase of St. Peter's Church" for a parish church and a plot of ground adjoining it as a burial-ground. The citizens, however, seemed to care but little for the gift, for nothing was done to make the roofless building fit for its proposed use for a period of twelve years. Then some slight repairs were done by an officer in the Army named Peter Chapman. Another quarter of a century elapsed, and then the east window was glazed, the choir was enclosed, but the nave was allowed still to remain without a roof.

It was not till Bishop Montague's time (1608–1616) that the building was completely roofed in.[1] Though Bishop Montague was translated to Winchester, yet when he

---

[1] The story of how Bishop Montague's attention was drawn to the condition of the church is told by Sir John Harrington. They were together in Bath and were caught in a heavy storm of rain, and the bishop asked Sir John to take him to some place of shelter. Sir John took him into the north aisle of the church. "We do not get much shelter here," said the bishop, to which Sir John replied, "If the church do not keep us safe from the water above, how shall it save others from the fire below."

died he was buried, not in the cathedral church of his new diocese, but in the church at Bath, where his monument may still be seen on the north side of the nave. Houses had grown up around the church, some actually abutting on the walls. The north aisle, at each end of which is a door, was for many years used as a public thoroughfare. A passage was afterwards cut through the houses on the north side, but it was not till about 1834 that the last house built against the church was removed. By this time the corporation was more alive to its duty than in the seventeenth century, and as the leases of the various houses fell in, pulled them down.

A good deal of money was spent about this time upon the fabric; flying buttresses were added to the nave, and pinnacles to the embattled turrets, at each end of the church. But a more complete restoration was set on foot during the incumbency of the Rev. Charles Kemble, under the direction of Sir Gilbert Scott. He, as was his habit, left the church in a thoroughly neat and trim condition. The nave and its aisles and the south transept were vaulted with stone, so as to match the roof of the choir, the plaster ceilings of Bishop Montague's time being removed to make place for them. The new roofs are thoroughly well executed, and all the carving is sharp and clear. In order to give an unbroken vista from end to end, the screen on which the organ stood was unfortunately removed, and the organ placed elsewhere. The galleries were also removed, and the numerous memorial tablets were taken from the positions they had previously occupied on walls and pillars, and were all neatly arranged along the walls beneath the string course that runs below the windows. At the present time (1901) restoration of a much to be regretted character is in progress on the exterior of the building. Fresh statues to take the place of mutilated and weathered ones are being set on the west front, and for many years to come will give the west front a spotty appearance, for their colour and sharpness will prevent them harmonising with the rest of the stone-work of the façade on which Time has left traces of his mellowing hands.

Photo.—T.P.

THE SOUTH TRANSEPT.

CHAPTER II.

BATH ABBEY occupies an excellent site, and may be well seen on all sides save the south, where houses approach it somewhat closely. The clearing away of the buildings which stood upon the site of the Roman baths has opened out a fine view from the south-west. The church consists of a nave with aisles; a central tower, oblong in plan; two narrow aisles, transepts, and a choir, with aisles projecting farther to the east than the east wall of the choir itself. The plan is perfectly symmetrical, the only excrescence being a vestry occupying the angle between the south transept and the choir aisle; this was built by Sir Nicholas Salterus.

The finest and most interesting part of the church is undoubtedly the **west front.** It has, moreover, the merit of being a genuine termination of the building behind it, not a mere screen for the display of statuary. At the angles of the nave are two turrets containing staircases. The two lower stages are rectangular; the upper, octagonal in plan; they rise above the parapet of the nave, and terminate in an embattled parapet, from within which rises a crocketed pyramid of eight sides—a modern addition. On the western faces of these turrets are carved the ladders mentioned in the last chapter. There are figures at their bases, which are seen, from old prints made when they were less dilapidated than at present, to be in attitudes of adoration. Figures of the twelve apostles under canopies are carved on the faces on either side of those faces of the two turrets that are decorated by the ladders and angels. The space above the large west window is occupied by carvings of angels and a large central figure under a canopy, no doubt intended to represent the Father; beneath this figure are several shields.

11

Some parts of the ladders have been renewed, but the upper parts have not been fully carved. On each ladder are two projecting blocks of stone, intended to be carved into figures of angels. The upper parts of the turrets have been altered from time to time. In a print of 1750 they appear much as at the present time; but from a later print we learn that the pyramidal terminations were not in existence in the early part of the nineteenth century. The great west window is one of seven lights divided horizontally into four parts. Below it is a battlemented parapet with a niche in the centre, in which, no doubt, a statue formerly stood, and in which a new statue has recently been placed. At the base of it are the arms and supporters of Henry VII. Below it is the west door, beneath a rectangular label. The spandrels contain emblems of the Passion. On either side stand statues of St. Peter and St. Paul, to whom the church was jointly dedicated; these seem to be of Elizabethan date. The doors themselves were the gift to the church of the Lord Chief Justice, Sir Henry Montague, brother of the bishop who completed the church. On them may be seen shields bearing the arms of the Montagues and of the Bishop of Bath and Wells. On the central mullion of the windows at the west ends of the two aisles is a canopied figure. Above the window of the north aisle are carved the words Domus mea, and above the window of the south aisle Domus oronis—an abbreviation for *orationis*. On the west faces of the buttresses at the corners of the aisles may be seen an olive rising through a crown and surmounted by a mitre—a rebus on the name and title of Bishop Oliver King; below are figures of animals much mutilated, beneath which may be read on a scroll portions of words from the parable of the trees choosing a king. Beneath the window at the west end of each aisle is a doorway, the head of which is a four-centred arch beneath a rectangular label.

The **nave** consists of five bays. The clerestory windows are unusually lofty, and are divided by transoms; they are of five lights. Along the top of the clerestory wall is a battlemented, pierced parapet; but the pattern of the pierced openings differs from that of the parapet which runs along the top of the aisle walls. The aisles have five-light windows without transoms; their heads are four centred arches; between each bay are projecting buttresses of three stages with gabled offsets, finished with crocketed pinnacles; against them rest flying buttresses formed of a lower semi-arch with a straight upper rectilinear truss, the character of which may best be understood by examination of the photograph, p. 10. From the points where

Photo.—T.P.

THE WEST FRONT.

the arched flying buttresses abut against the clerestory walls, vertical, slightly projecting buttresses are built upwards against the wall and, rising above the parapet, are finished by crocketed pinnacles. The same design is carried right round the church.

The clerestory of the transepts resembles those of the nave and choir.

The **central tower** is not square, but oblong in plan, the east and west sides being considerably longer than those on the south and north. It rises two stages above the roof. In each face are two pairs of windows with rectangular heads. Those of the lower stage have transoms, and are blocked up; those on the upper story have no transoms, and are furnished with louvre boards. At each angle of the tower is a massive octagonal turret somewhat similar to those on the north-west and south-west angles of the nave. At the ends of the transepts are lofty windows, which are crossed by three transoms. The buttresses, pinnacles, and windows of the choir, which consists of three bays, resemble the corresponding parts of the nave.

At the north-east and south-east angles of the **choir** are two turrets, square in section until they reach the level of the parapet, and octagonal above, terminating in octagonal pyramids decorated with crockets similar to those which may be seen on the turrets of the tower. The great east window of the choir is of seven lights, aud its body is divided by transoms into four tiers. It is set under a rectangular head, the spandrels between the arch of the window proper being pierced by foliated arches and smaller openings. The aisles, as already mentioned, project beyond the east wall of the choir to a distance equal to about half a bay. It is possible that it was originally intended to throw out a lady-chapel between them. The north wall of the projecting part of the north aisle and the corresponding wall of the south aisle are furnished with buttresses, but there is no window between them. There are four-light windows at the east end of each of the choir aisles, with a small door below them.

It only remains to mention the low vestry built against the east wall of the south transept, having its greatest length from north to south, and a small door in the wall of the middle bay of the south choir aisle, and the date 1576 cut on the south side of the buttress, which projects southward from the south-east corner of the south transept: this probably gives the date of the completion of some work of repair on this part of the building. It will be noticed that this date is sixteen years later than the time when the church was presented to the city by Edmund Colthurst. Some remains of the tower piers of John de Villula's church may be seen rising about a foot or so above the ground against the eastern buttresses.

Although compared with many abbey churches Bath is of small dimensions; although its details are in many respects poor; although it has not those various irregularities and surprises that one meets with in examining those churches which have been the growth of centuries, and were altered and added to as occasion and the changed circumstances of the times required—features which lend such a charm and interest to many old buildings;—yet it cannot be denied that it is a well-proportioned building, and that even its exterior is not devoid of dignity and beauty; and when we pass into the interior, the general effect will be found still more impressive.

THE NAVE, LOOKING EAST.

CHAPTER III.

THE general view of the interior of Bath Abbey Church from the west end is very fine. The vault of the nave rises to about 75 ft. ; and as the span is about 32 ft., it will be seen that the ratio of height to width is about 2·3 to 1—rather above the average of English churches. But the height of the building seems greater than it really is, as there is but one horizontal line dividing the walls of the nave and choir—a string course running above the arches of the main arcading and below the tall clerestory windows, whose sills are brought down to it. There is no triforium. The building is exceedingly well lighted,—so bright, indeed, was the interior on account of the large size of the windows and the absence of painted glass that the church received the name of the "Lantern of the West." The flood of light has now been somewhat subdued by the introduction of painted glass into nearly all the windows of the nave and choir aisles, as well as into three of the four large windows of the church, and by a colour wash of a light green tint applied to the clerestory windows on the south side. The windows of the clerestory right round the building have five lights, and are divided horizontally by one transom ; those of the north and south side in the aisles have five lights without any transom. The great east and west windows have seven lights ; the west one is divided by two, the eastern by three transoms. The windows at the north and south side of the transepts have five lights, and are divided by two transoms. In all cases besides the transoms there is practically another horizontal division just below the head of the window, formed by the heads of the lights below it. The tracery, as will be seen from the illustrations, is thoroughly Perpendicular in character; but only in the east and west windows do any of the mullions run in an unbroken line from the sills to the containing arch; in these two windows the mullion on each side of the central light is so continued. A detailed description of the subjects of painted glass may be interesting to some visitors, so it is here given.

The Windows.—Most of the lower windows are filled with modern painted glass. The tracery, of course, is Perpendicular in character, and that of one window bears an almost exact resemblance to that of all the rest. There is, however, one minute difference to be seen; if we count the clerestory windows from the west right through the nave and choir, we find that the heads of the lower lights are foliated in all the windows that bear an even number, while the corresponding lights in the other four windows on each side are plain. The clerestory windows on the east side of the north transept have lower lights with plain heads, while those on the west of this transept and on both sides of the south transept have the heads of the corresponding lights foliated.

Beginning with the west window of the north aisle, and going along the north aisles of nave and choir and back to the west end by the south choir and nave aisles, we note the subjects of the various windows, the persons to whose memory they were inserted, and the name of the firms that designed and produced them.

The window over the north-west door contains figures of the four Evangelists. It is a memorial window to Charles Empson, who died in 1861. It is by Chance, and both in drawing and colour is the worst window in the church.

The first window on the north side represents Hannah praying for a son, the finding of Moses, Ruth and Boaz, Martha and Mary, Christ and Mary, and the two Marys at the sepulchre. It was inserted by T. Gill in memory of his daughter, Louisa Gignac Waring, and is by Clayton & Bell.

The second window contains emblems of the four Evangelists and sundry arms and mottoes. It is a memorial to various members of the St. Barbe family. Much old glass was employed in its construction by Clayton & Bell, who added some glass of their own painting to complete it.

The third window, in memory of John Soden, represents

various incidents in the life of John the Baptist. It is by Clayton & Bell.

The fourth window, in memory of Colonel Madox, who died in 1865, represents Christ's charge to His disciples (Luke xxiv.). This is by Ward & Hughes.

The fifth represents the raising of the widow's son by Elijah, the sea giving up its dead, the raising of the son of the Widow of Nain, Samuel and Eli, the Good Shepherd, Timothy taught by Lois, and Isaac, Josiah, David, and Joseph, and was inserted by the late vicar, Mr. Kemble, in memory of a son who was drowned in the Bay of Tunis; it was made by Clayton & Bell.

We now cross the transept.

The first window of the choir, in memory of Edmund Barrow Evans, who died in 1868, represents Christ preaching on the mount, and is by Bell of Bristol.

The second window, in memory of the Rev. Henry Barrow Evans, who died in 1856, represents Christ reading in the synagogue, and is by Bell of Bristol.

The third window represents the miracle at Cana in Galilee, and also contains figures of the Virgin and Child, Eve and her sons, Sarah and Isaac, Elizabeth and John, Hannah and Samuel. It was erected to the memory of Lieutenant-Colonel Jackson Doveton, who died in 1868, and is by Clayton & Bell.

The window at the east end of this aisle contains representations of the Nativity, Baptism, Crucifixion, and Ascension. It was put up as a memorial to Humphrey Newman, an ensign, by his brother officers, and was painted by O'Connell.

The corresponding window of the south choir aisle contains the figures of the four Evangelists. It was presented by two sisters of the name of Jamieson, and is by O'Connell.

The easternmost window of the south choir aisle is of white glass.

The next, containing various subjects—Jeremiah, Christ among the doctors, and the doves being offered in the Temple—is in memory of William Gomm, of St. Petersburg, who died in 1792, and was inserted in 1870. It was painted by Burlison & Grylls. Under this window is a narrow doorway.

The westernmost window on the south side of this aisle is of Munich glass, and represents the miraculous draught of fishes and St. Paul preaching at Athens. It is a memorial window to William Wildman Kettlewell, who died in 1872.

Under this window is a doorway, not, however, placed beneath its centre.

Crossing the transept, we enter the east end of the south aisle of the nave.

The first window represents the adoration of the Wise Men and scenes from the life of the Virgin. It is in memory of James H. Markland, who died in 1864.

The next represents the miraculous draught of fishes (John xxi. 11), in memory of Admiral Norwich Duff, who died in 1860, and is by Ward & Hughes.

The third, in memory of George Norman, F.R.G.S., who died in 1861, is by Clayton & Bell, and represents Christ healing the sick.

The fourth represents Moses with the tables of the Law, and also contains figures of Charity, Faith, Justice, and Hope. It is in memory of Edward F. Slack, who died in 1817, and is by Clayton & Bell. Under this window is a doorway, not central.

The last window, in memory of Robert Arthur Brooke, who died in 1860, represents the raising of the son of the Widow of Nain, the healing of the centurion's servant, Christ blessing little children, the exhortation to watch and pray, and the question respecting the tribute money. It is by Ward & Hughes.

The window at the west end of this aisle represents the four builders, Moses, David, Solomon, and Zerubbabel. It is by Bell, and was given by the contractors who carried out the restoration in 1864.

The great east window contains representations of various incidents in the life of Christ. It was presented to the church by the members of the Bath Literary Club, and is by Clayton & Bell.

The west window of the nave contains various subjects from Old Testament history. This window was not filled' with painted glass all at the same time. In 1888 the north side was inserted as a memorial to Bartlett and Jane Little and six of their children. The other lights have now been filled. The glass is by Clayton & Bell.

The windows at the north and south ends of the transept are tall and narrow, five-light windows crossed by three transoms. The clerestory windows have also five lights, but are crossed by one transom only. There is no painted glass in the north transept. The window at the end of the south transept is a Jesse window. In the lower lights we find the sickness and recovery of Hezekiah, together with the royal arms, those of the Prince and Princess of Wales, and those of the city of Bath. The painted glass was inserted to commemorate the recovery of the present King from his serious illness in 1872, when he was Prince of Wales. It is by Clayton & Bell.

Of the two lower windows of this transept, the western one has white glass, the eastern one is painted with the following subjects : " I was an hungred, and ye gave Me meat " ; " Suffer little children to come unto Me " ; " Visit the fatherless." It is a memorial window to Richard Brooke, who died in 1875.

No church, save St. Peter's, Westminster, has so many **Monuments** of the dead as this. It is said that there are more than six hundred memorial tablets, besides a few statues. At one time these were stuck on every point of vantage, walls and piers alike ; but when the church was restored they were all tidily placed beneath the string course below the aisle windows, and so thickly are these parts of the walls covered with them that it would be hard to find room for the erection of many more. For the most part, they are of little interest to anyone save the relatives of the persons whose names and virtues they were erected to commemorate. The great number of these tablets may be accounted for by the fact that Bath was during the eighteenth century a great centre of fashionable life, and that it was then, and has been ever since it ceased to hold its own against other resorts of fashion, a spot to which invalids are attracted by the real or supposed beneficial effects of its hot baths and mineral waters. Many of these seekers after pleasure or health died at Bath, and, as they were for the most part drawn from the wealthy classes, tablets were erected to their memory in the abbey. The numerous monuments of the dead gave rise to the well-known couplet :

> " These walls, so full of monument and bust,
> Show how Bath waters serve to lay the dust."

Only a few of the monuments need be mentioned. The place of honour in the list must be given to the altar tomb of Bishop Montague, who, as recorded in Chapter I., did so much towards the completion of the fabric, and who died as Bishop of

Winchester in 1618. This tomb may be seen under the fourth arch of the nave arcading on the north side.

BISHOP MONTAGUE'S TOMB.   *Photo.—T.P.*

Under the southern window of the transept is a striking monument to the wife of Sir William Waller, the well-known general in the time of the Civil Wars, who commanded the Parliamentary forces in the Battle of Landsdown, close to Bath. In the front lies the figure of the dead lady, her face turned somewhat

LADY WALLER'S MONUMENT.   *Photo.—T.P.*

inwards. Between her and the wall her living husband, clad in mail, reclines on his right elbow, gazing down on his wife's face. Behind the figures, under semicircular arches, are two spaces for inscriptions. That on the western side is blank ; it was probably intended to receive the epitaph of Sir William, but he died and was buried in London. The other bears the following inscription :

> " To the deare
> Memory of the right
> Vertuous and worthy lady
> JANE LADY WALLER sole daughter
> And heire to Sr Richard Reynell
> And wife to Sr William Waller k^t.
>
> Sole issue of a matchlesse paire
> Both of their state and vertues heyre
> In graces great, in stature small
> As full of spirit as voyd of gall
> Cheerfully brave bounteously close
> Holy without vain glorious showes
> Happy and yet from envy free
> Learn'd without pride witty yet wise
> Reader this riddle read with mee
> Here the good Lady Waller lyes."

At the head and feet of the lady two weeping children kneel.

To the south side of the altar, on the wall facing north, is a monument to Bartholomew Barnes and his wife. Both figures are represented kneeling, with hands clasped for prayer, facing each other—he to the east, she to the west. Beneath him kneels the small figure of one son, and beneath her kneel five daughters. Its date is 1608.

In the south side of the north choir aisle, towards its eastern end, is a tablet erected to the memory of the actor Quin, with an inscription by Garrick. Near the altar, on its north side, is the elder Bacon's monument of Lady Miller. On the south side of the western door of the nave is a monument to Colonel Champion, by Nollekens. On the opposite side of the door is a monument to Herman Katencamp, by the younger Bacon, dated 1807. In the south aisle is a tablet to William Hoare, R.A., by Chantrey. Another, by the same sculptor, may be seen in the choir aisle in memory of Admiral Sir Richard Bickerton. There are two monuments by Flaxman—one to the Hon. W. Bingham in the south aisle of the nave, and the other to Dr. Sibthorp, botanist, in the south choir aisle. Dr. Sibthorp is represented with a bunch of botanical specimens, just gathered, in his hand.

The story of the Good Samaritan appears in more than one place in high relief on tablets erected to the memory of physicians. The most conspicuous one may be seen on the east wall of the south transept in memory of Jacob Bosanquet, who died in 1767.

Photo.—T.P.

COLONEL ALEXANDER CHAMPION'S MONUMENT BY NOLLEKENS.

The most beautiful piece of work in the church is **Prior Birde's Chantry** (see page 7), between the choir and its south aisle, under the easternmost arch of the arcading. It is most elaborately carved, and the rebus of the founder—a W and a Bird—appears upon it in several places. It consists of two bays. The whole of the western bay and the southern half of

the eastern bay are vaulted with fan tracery.   The vaulting at
the eastern end is different.   On this vaulting may be seen
Prior Birde's arms, and above them a mitre and pastoral staff.
    There is a little variety in the arches and shafts throughout

Photo.—T.P.

THE NAVE, SOUTH SIDE.

the church.   This repetition is a well-known feature in **Perpendicular** work.   The piers have no general capital.   The shaft
which carries the inner order of the arch has a capital, and so,
at the same level, have the vaulting shafts of the high vault and

that of the aisles. These shafts spring from the bases of the main pillars. The capitals at this level are plain, and so are the capitals of the vaulting shafts of the nave from which the vaulting ribs spring. But in the choir the place of these plain bands is taken by carved angels. Carved angels also form the termination of the hood moulding of the lower windows of the south transept, and probably of those of the north transept also, though these windows are hidden by the wooden pipes of the organ.

Over the heads of the clerestory windows of the nave are small shields, and shields may also be seen in the centre of the fan tracery in the nave, choir, and transept. In the aisles the fan tracery is somewhat different, as in the centre of each bay there is a pendant. As has already been mentioned, the vaulting of the nave and its aisles and that of the south transept are modern, put up, under the direction of Sir Gilbert Scott, to match the roof of the choir and its aisles and north transept respectively. The reredos was designed by the same architect. The oak screen across the eastern part of the south choir aisle is due to his son. The font is also modern. In fact, beyond the walls and the roofing of the eastern part of the church, there is little old about it. In the clerestory windows are a few fragments of seventeenth-century glass—heraldic shields.

The floor of the present church is about six feet higher than that of John de Villula's church; and during the restoration some portions of the foundations of this church were discovered, enough to learn something of its dimensions. Just within the west wall are remains of part of the north jamb of the great west doorway, and in the south aisle a small piece of a column. In the north aisle of the nave, near the second pillar from the west and also near the next pillar to the east, are the foundations of two Norman piers. Their position shows that the span of the central nave was wider than at present; and if, as is probable, the aisle walls of Bishop King's church occupy the same position as the aisle walls of its predecessor, the Norman aisles must have been narrower. The foundations of another Norman pier exist near the first pillar on the north side of the choir, counting from the east. And at the extreme east end, outside the eastern buttresses on both sides, are remains of what were probably the western piers of the central tower. The foundations of the choir of the Norman church, if they exist, are buried below the surface of the open space and roads to the east of the church. The head of the east window of the south choir aisle, it may be added, is semicircular. Gratings have been placed over some fragments of the foundations of the Norman church to allow of their being inspected.

The position of the vestry was described in the last chapter. It is a comfortable-looking room with an ornamental plaster ceiling, and contains some of the original copperplates from which the illustrations of J. Britton's book on Bath were printed.

The **Organ** is a very fine one, erected in 1895; it is placed in the transept. The wooden pipes are arranged against the walls of the north transept, rising from the floor and hiding some of the windows; the metal pipes are placed beneath the north and south arches of the tower, at some height above the floor. At present they are not contained in any organ-case; but a design for one has been made, and money is being collected for defraying the cost of its erection. All the newest principles of construction are embodied in the organ. The air is conveyed by gas-piping from the wind-chest to the organ-pipes.

The bells of the abbey were sold at the time of the dissolution of the monastery, but it is possible that they were re-purchased for the church by the parish; at any rate, the church was, during the sixteenth century, furnished with six bells, the largest a very heavy one. In 1700 these six bells were melted, and from the metal was cast a peal of eight bells; and in 1774 two more were added, making the number up to ten. In 1890 machinery was added by which at 1 p.m., 5 p.m., and 9 p.m. chimes are played; these are different on each day of the week, the series forming a strange mixture of sacred and secular tunes, as will be seen from the following list:

Sunday: "The Easter hymn."
Monday: "Stella."
Tuesday: "The harp that once in Tara's halls."
Wednesday: "All Saints."
Thursday: "Ye Banks and Braes of Bonny Doon."
Friday: "Come, ye faithful."
Saturday: "Tom Bowling."

CHAPTER IV.

THE PRIORS OF BATH.

IT will not be necessary to give a list of the bishops of Bath and Wells, as this may be found in the volume on Wells in Bell's "Cathedral Series." The first of the Somerset bishops connected with Bath was John, a monk from Tours, who from his medical skill made large sums of money, and with it purchased of the king the ruins of the town of Bath, which had been burnt during the insurrection of Odo, Bishop of Bayeux, in the reign of William Rufus. He rebuilt the abbey church and constituted it the seat of his diocese. From this time forward the bishop was the abbot; but only a few of his immediate successors followed the example of John de Villula in residing at Bath, and Wells became once again the chief residence of the bishops who bore the title of Bath and Wells. Hence the prior became the virtual head of the monastery. The names of most of the priors from the time of John de Villula are preserved. In some cases record exists of the dates of their appointments; in other cases we simply find them mentioned as priors of Bath in connection with some special historical event.

A certain JOHN was prior in the days of Bishop John de Villula.

PETER was elected in 1159, and is mentioned in 1175.

WALTER died in 1198.

HUGH is mentioned as prior in 1190. He appears to have been acting in place of Walter, who was for a time absent from Bath.

ROBERT is mentioned as prior in 1198, when he probably succeeded Walter.

THOMAS is mentioned as prior in 1228, and died in 1261.

29

WALTER DE AONA succeeded Thomas in 1261, and was still prior in 1275.

THOMAS DE WYNTON was elected in 1291, and resigned in 1301.

ROBERT DE CLOPPECOTE was no doubt at once elected, as he is mentioned as prior in 1303. He has the unenviable reputation of being an oppressor of the monks. He died in 1331.

ROBERT DE SUTTON was elected by the monks in 1331, but the pope would not sanction his appointment.

THOMAS CHRISTI was appointed prior by the Pope, but he resigned in 1332.

Another ROBERT is mentioned as prior in 1333.

JOHN DE IFORD, Prior of Bath, was charged with adultery in 1346, and either resigned or was deprived of his office in consequence.

JOHN DE BEREWIKE, or John de Berkelye, is mentioned as prior in 1363, and again in 1370.

JOHN DE FORDE was prior in 1371.

JOHN DE WALCOTE succeeded him.

Another prior JOHN died in 1412.

JOHN DE TELESFORD was elected in 1412, and died in 1425.

WILLIAM SOUTHBROKE was elected in 1426, and died in 1447.

THOMAS LAYCOCK was holding the office in 1451.

RICHARD is mentioned as prior in 1476.

JOHN CANTLOW was elected in 1498, and died in 1499.

WILLIAM BIRDE, who has been mentioned in connection with the rebuilding of the abbey, was elected in 1499, and held the post till his death in 1525.

WILLIAM HOLLOWAY, or GYBBS, succeeded him, and carried on the work of rebuilding; but he was obliged to surrender the abbey in 1539, and consequently was the last of the priors of Bath.

MALMESBURY ABBEY CHURCH.

THE CONVENTUAL
SEAL OF
MALMESBURY ABBEY.

MALMESBURY ABBEY FROM THE SOUTH.

MALMESBURY ABBEY CHURCH.

CHAPTER I.

HISTORY OF THE BUILDING.

THE little town of Malmesbury stands on a lofty promontory or peninsula, for two streams, the Bristol Avon and Newnton Water, flowing in a southerly direction, almost meet, leaving but a narrow ridge of ground between them, then separate again, to unite finally a little farther to the south. On the narrow neck of land just mentioned stands the suburb of Westport; across the narrowest part no doubt in former times ran a rampart or wall, and the name Westport keeps alive the memory of a fortified gateway which defended the town on the north-western side. The quadrangular space enclosed by the two rivers is occupied by the town of Malmesbury. The abbey was built at the southern end of the ridge, just where it opens out into the quadrangle mentioned above, and looked out to the north from the edge of the escarpment which rises above Newnton Water.

The early history of the town is shrouded in the dim mist of legend. One Dunwal Maelmutius, or Malmud, King Paramount of Britain, father of that Brennus of whom we read in Roman history as having forced his way into the city of Rome in the days of Camillus, is said to have founded, about the year 400 B.C., a city where Malmesbury now stands. Other chronicles speak of the existence, even in earlier times than this, of an encampment on the high ground between the Avon and Newnton Water. That such a stronghold did exist is by no means improbable, since the character of the place would naturally suggest it as being eminently suitable for defence. It

is said that its original name was Bladon. Of its condition
during the time of the Roman occupation of Britain we have
no written record, nor have any Roman remains been found in
the immediate neighbourhood. When the Teutonic tribes
invaded Britain, the Keltic inhabitants fled from Bladon, and
it became an important military post under the name of
Ingleburne, and, standing as it did on the borders of Wessex
and Mercia, it was sometimes held by one, sometimes by the
other of these two rival powers that fought for the supremacy
of the island. A nunnery is said to have existed here in the
fifth century of the Christian era ; if so, the nunnery was in all
probability destroyed and the nuns driven out or slain by the
heathen conquerors. Leland, however, speaks of a nunnery
existing near the Castle of Ingleburne at a somewhat later date,
and tells us that the nuns, having been guilty of acts of
unchastity with the garrison, were expelled by the Saxon
archbishop. He also says that the nuns were under the
direction of Dinoth, Abbot of Bangor. All this is, however,
very uncertain. The first authentic figure that emerges from the
mist of legend is one Maldulf, from whose name, according to
some authorities, the word Malmesbury was derived, though
another derivation is Mal-dunes-bury, the City of the Hill of the
Cross. Maldulf is sometimes spoken of as an Irishman, sometimes as a Scot. Possibly he was one of the Scots who
remained in their old home in Ireland when the main body
of the tribe migrated to Caledonia, to which they gave the
name of Scotland. Ireland in these early days was the home
of religion and learning, and it was by Irish missionaries that
Christianity was first introduced into the south of Scotland and
north of England.

Maldulf is spoken of as a hermit. What brought him to
Malmesbury we do not know. Finding the wild woodland
to his taste, he made up his mind to settle here. The palace
and manor of the petty king of the district were hard by at a
spot known as Caer-dur-burh. Of this chieftain Maldulf asked
and obtained permission to build for himself a cell under
Caer-Bladon, the stronghold on the river Bladon, now known
by the name Avon. Maldulf was extremely poor, if we may
trust William of Malmesbury, who says, "Deficientibus
necessariis scholares in disciplinam accepit, ut eorum liber-
alitate tenuitatem victus corrigeret." The pupils who were

attracted by his learning were formed in course of time into a "monasterium," by which we must understand not a fully developed *monastery*, but a little band of disciples living together and looking up with reverence to the wisdom of their master. The most distinguished among the pupils was the famous Ealdhelm, who was of near kin to Ine, the West Saxon king. He may be regarded as the real founder of the Abbey of Malmesbury ; before his death he became Bishop of Sherborne, when the great West Saxon diocese was divided about 705 A.D.

It is impossible to give the exact date of the coming of Maldulf to Malmesbury ; all we can be sure of was that he came during the latter half of the seventh century. There was a deed, which William of Malmesbury incorporated in the chronicles, in which Leotherius, or Eleutherius, who was Bishop of Wessex from 672 to 676, made a grant of land for the foundation of an abbey. If this document were genuine, the date of the formal foundation is brought within very narrow limits ; but documents of this nature may be looked upon with some suspicion. It has indeed been suggested that many such deeds purporting to make grants of land to religious houses were forged by the monks at the time of the Norman Conquest in order that they might not be despoiled of their land by William I., who, despite many unchristian acts, yet wished to stand well with the Church. The great West Saxon King Alfred wrote a life of Ealdhelm, but unfortunately this has perished, and we have only the chronicle of Faricius, a monk of Malmesbury, who became Abbot of Abingdon in 1100 A.D., and that of William of Malmesbury, who wrote about 1140 A.D., from which to gather details of his life.

Both these men—with the view of exalting the honour of their religious house, of which Ealdhelm was practically the founder, though nominally the second abbot, Maldulf being considered the first—interwove with the real events of his life many legends, some of which, on account of their miraculous character, we can reject at once, but others we can only mark as doubtful. Among the former is one closely resembling that told of the miraculous beam at Christchurch Priory, Hants. It is said that when Ealdhelm was superintending the building of his church one of the beams was too short for its purpose, and was lengthened in answer to the abbot's prayer, and that it afterwards remained unscathed, though twice in after years the roof of the church was destroyed by fire. It is also said that the ruins of the church that he built were never wet with the rains of heaven, even in the stormiest weather; it is also recorded that on one occasion when he knelt down to pray he hung his outer garment on a sunbeam, from which it hung suspended as though upon a clothes-line. Among the stories about Ealdhelm that we may believe is the following. The abbot, having noticed that the country people cared little to listen to any preachers of Christianity, however eloquent they might be, while at the same time they delighted exceedingly in music, stationed himself on a bridge over which many wayfarers had to pass, and there played upon a harp and sang songs that were popular favourites of the day, and then, having thus gathered a crowd round him, he changed the character of his lays and began to sing psalms and hymns and spiritual songs, and thus led the people to listen to the truths he desired to teach. This anecdote is related by William of Malmesbury, and he says he obtained it from King Alfred's life of the saint.

Apart from all monkish exaggeration it may be safely asserted that Ealdhelm was a man of distinguished piety and virtue. The year of his birth is uncertain. William of Malmesbury speaks of him as a lad (*pusio*) in 670, but his name appears as one of the attesting witnesses to a Glastonbury charter dated 670, and in this he signs his name as "Ealdhelm Abbas." Again it is stated that he was Abbot of Malmesbury for thirty years, and that at the time of his death, which certainly occurred in 709 A.D., he was seventy years of age.

The grant of land for the purpose of founding an abbey contains some rather singular clauses. Eleutherius seems to fear that in future times disputes would arise between the monks and the bishops, for he says that he makes the grant with hesitation, and because he has been earnestly entreated to do so; and he expresses a hope that if trouble should arise, his successors will not lay the blame on him. When he appoints Ealdhelm abbot, he says he does so after due deliberation, and gives him authority to rule the abbey with the same power as that possessed by bishops. The deed then goes on to say that the bishop bestows on Ealdhelm, the priest, in order that he may lead a life according to strict rule, that portion of land called Maildulfesburg, in which place his earliest infancy had been passed and his first initiation in the study of learning had been received, and where he had been instructed in the liberal arts, and had passed his days nurtured in the bosom of Holy Mother Church. In the Malmesbury chartulary this deed bears the date 675 A.D. William of Malmesbury, however, dates the appointment three years earlier. But if we assume 675 to be the correct date, it will leave thirty years as the time he ruled the abbey before his appointment to the Bishopric of Sherborne in 705. Soon after its foundation the abbey began to receive endowments, both from the Mercian and the West Saxon kings, and the money so obtained gave Ealdhelm the means of building. On the foundations of an old church within the monastic precincts he raised a church dedicated to the Holy Saviour and the Apostles Peter and Paul; he also built within the precincts another church dedicated to St. Mary, and hard by a chapel to the honour of the Archangel Michael. Of this chapel William of Malmesbury says a few traces remained in his day, but of St. Mary's Church he says that it surpassed in size and beauty all other old churches in England, and adds some words, about the exact meaning of which there has been much dispute—namely, "Celebris et illibata nostro quoque perstitit ævo." But Ealdhelm built not only at Malmesbury, but also erected the little church at Bradford-on-Avon which was standing in the days of William of Malmesbury and still stands, the oldest church in England of whose building we have any authentic record. He also established a monastery at Frome, of which he was abbot.

When Ealdhelm died in 709 his body was laid in St. Michael's Chapel adjoining St. Mary's Church. The monks now used this church for their services, though the church of the Holy Saviour and the Apostles Peter and Paul was still regarded as *caput loci*, or chief church. A silver shrine to contain the good abbot's bones was presented to the abbey by King Ethelwulf; on the outside of this might be seen in low relief representations of the miracles that he is recorded to have worked.

Alfred, the great West Saxon king, though he gave no grant of money or land to the abbey, attempted to raise its position as a seat of learning, but in this attempt he signally failed. He sent to Malmesbury a learned Scot, John by name, who was the author of a treatise on the "Division of Nature." But this John met with little favour as a teacher; and the pupils of the monastery school stabbed him with the steel instruments that they used for writing, so that he died. We are not told what was the special reason for his unpopularity; it may be that he attempted to make idle pupils work against their will, it may be that his coming was resented as the intrusion of a stranger. Anyhow, he was murdered; but it came to pass that after his death he was regarded as a martyr, and his body was buried in the Church of the Holy Saviour and the Apostles Peter and Paul.

The greatest of all the royal benefactors to Malmesbury town and abbey was Alfred's grandson, Athelstan. "What Harold was to Waltham," says Professor Freeman, "Waltheof to Crowland, Simon de Montfort to Evesham, 'Glorious' Æthelstan was to the no less venerable pile of Malmesbury." It seems that in one of the numerous battles between the English and the Danes the inhabitants of Malmesbury bore themselves like men, and gave valuable help to Athelstan. In consequence of this he made the burgesses a grant of land which they still enjoy. There are now 280 allotments of 2 acres, 48 of 3 acres, 24 of 4 acres, and 12 of 10 acres. And on the marriage of one of those entitled to receive the grant, he is taken to the piece of land which falls to him, and the steward hands to him a turf cut from the soil, and gives him three strokes across his back with a twig cut from his allotment, at the same time uttering the words:

> " Turf and twig I give to thee
> Same as King Athelstan gave to me."

No stranger coming to Malmesbury, however long he may reside there, can obtain an allotment; none but the sons of former holders or one who marries a daughter of a former holder can obtain the grant, and no unmarried man can claim it. The names of those eligible for it are entered on a list, and they are appointed in rotation; and when vacancies

occur, those who hold a two-acre plot are promoted to a
three-acre plot, and so on. The holders may not build on the
land, nor does the holding convey any political or municipal
rights.

Among other valuable gifts, King Athelstan gave to the
abbey two most precious relics—a portion of the Holy
Cross and a thorn from the Crown of Thorns. No wonder
that the possession of such priceless treasures brought pilgrims

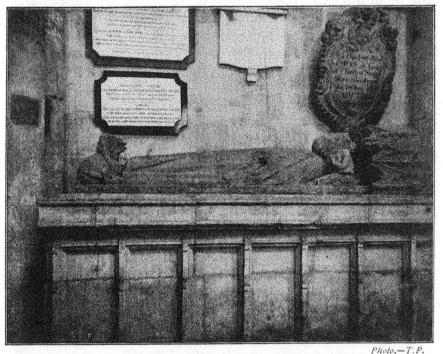

Photo.—T.P.

SUPPOSED TOMB OF ATHELSTAN.

to the abbey. Moreover, when two of Athelstan's nephews
were slain in battle with the Danes, he brought their bodies
and buried them at the head of the tomb of their sainted
kinsman Ealdhelm, and when he himself lay a-dying at
Gloucester he desired that his remains should be borne to
Malmesbury. Here he was buried in a spot which it is hard
to identify. William of Malmesbury says " he was buried
under the altar of St. Mary in the tower, wherefore they are
wrong who say that the Abbot Ælfric built the tower, since

he was not appointed abbot until thirty years after Athelstan's death." But in " De Gestis Regum " the same writer asserts that " he was buried at the head of the sepulchre of St. Ealdhelm "—that is, in St. Michael's Chapel. Are we from the contradictory nature of these two assertions to come to the conclusion that William is not accurate in his details, or can we reconcile them by supposing that he is speaking in the former passage of the spot to which Ealdhelm's bones were afterwards removed when Dunstan, in fear of the Danes, took them from the silver shrine in St. Michael's Chapel and laid them in St. Mary's Church?

King Edwy was no lover of monks, and he showed his hatred of them at Malmesbury by expelling them and putting secular clergy in their place, turning the monastery, as one of the injured monks says, into "a sty of secular canons." The monks, however, retained possession of the bones of Ealdhelm, who had been dead some two hundred and fifty years, and showed them to the king as they lay within the silver shrine, on whose crystal cover the saint's name shone in letters of gold. Whereupon Edwy, out of respect to the memory of his illustrious kinsman, restored the monks to their former place, and moreover bestowed on them the Manor of Brokenborough, one of the most valuable gifts they had yet received.

In the reign of Edgar the Peaceful things looked brighter for monks throughout the land. In a document dated 974 this king says: "Considering what offering I should make from my earthly kingdom to the King of kings, I resolve to rebuild all the holy monasteries throughout my kingdom, which as they are outwardly ruinous with mouldering shingles and worm-eaten boards even to the rafters, so what is still worse, they have been internally. neglected and almost destitute of the service of God. Wherefore ejecting those illiterate clerks (*i.e.,* the secular clergy) subject to the discipline of no regular order, in many places I have appointed pastors of a holier race that is of the monastic order, supplying them with ample means out of my royal revenues to repair their churches wherever dilapidated. One of these pastors by name Ælfric I have appointed guardian of that most celebrated monastery which the Angles call by the twofold name Maldelmsburg." We may here notice that this peculiar form of the name seems to have been formed by combining the names of Maldulf and Ealdhelm.

There are conflicting accounts of the architectural work carried out by the Abbot Ælfric. William of Malmesbury, when speaking of Athelstan's time, says: "It may be necessary to observe that at that time the Church of St. Peter was the chief of the monastery which now (that is, about 1140) is deemed second only; the Church of St. Mary, which the monks at present frequent, was built afterwards, in the reign of Edgar, under Abbot Ælfric." But it is not clear whether we should regard Ælfric's work as an entire rebuilding or as a restoration of St. Mary's Church. Certain it is that St. Mary's now became the chief church, although the smaller Church of St. Peter and St. Paul, once the *caput loci*, seems to have stood until the dissolution; for Leland, who was at Malmesbury in 1540, in his description of what he saw there, says: "There was a little church joining the south side of the transept of the abbey church in which some said that John the Scot, the preceptor, was slain by his pupils in the time of King Alfred—weavers have now their looms in this little church, but it standeth and is a very old piece of work."

It is recorded that Dunstan gave to the new or restored Church of St. Mary a large organ with pipes of metal and a brass plate, whereon was an inscription in Latin verse of his own composing. But this was not the first organ that the abbey possessed, for one had been built under the direction of Ealdhelm, who himself described it as a mighty instrument of innumerable tones, blown with bellows and enclosed in a gilded case. This is the first instance on record of an organ being used in England.

Dunstan, as has been mentioned above, removed the body of Ealdhelm from its shrine and placed it in a stone tomb at the right-hand side of the high altar in St. Mary's Church.

During the time of Ethelred II. the monks suffered in many ways; the heathen Danes obtained a footing in the country, and destroyed churches and monasteries. A party of marauders attacked the church at Malmesbury, and one of them tried to break off the precious stones from the shrine of St. Ealdhelm, but fell back as though shot; whereupon the rest fled, and so Malmesbury escaped the destruction

that overtook many other religious houses at that time.   On
another occasion two Danish chieftains were seized and put
to death by order of Ethelred ; the widow of one of them
was carried a prisoner to " Malmcestre," as the chronicler
Langtoft spells the name.   This lady was young and endowed
with great beauty, and when Edmund, the king's son, afterwards known as " Ironside," heard thereof, he straightway
took horse and rode to Malmesbury, and there and then
wedded her without his father's knowledge.

During the reigns of Cnut and his two sons little is heard
of Malmesbury save that one Constantine, a refugee archbishop, became a monk of Malmesbury, and planted a vineyard
for the monks to make wine for themselves withal, of the
quality of which, however, no record has come down to us.

In the year 1059, when Edward the Confessor was king,
Abbot Brithwald was buried, as many of his predecessors
had been, so says William, in the Church of St. Andrew.
As this church is not elsewhere mentioned, it may be that
St. Andrew is a *lapsus calami* on the part of the chronicler
for St. Michael, a chapel in which we know that Ealdhelm
was buried, and probably some of his successors, who would
naturally wish that their bones should lie as close as possible
to those of the great saint.   Be this as it may, the dead
abbots were greatly incensed that Brithwald, who had not
been a holy man, should make his grave with them, and
their ghosts began to disturb the monks, until they decided
to dig up the unwelcome intruder's body and to cast it into
a marsh outside the abbey precincts.   When this was done,
the dead abbots' ghosts walked no more.   It was during
the vacancy caused by his death that Herman, a Fleming
who had been the king's chaplain, and had been appointed
Bishop of the Diocese of the Wilisætas, and had his bishop-
stool in the cathedral church, which stood at what we now
call Old Sarum, near Salisbury, sought to unite the Abbey
of Malmesbury with all its revenues to the episcopal see.
Edward the king gave his consent to this arrangement ; but
the monks strongly resisted the attempt to absorb their abbey,
just as in after times the monks of Glastonbury objected to
the incorporation of their abbey in the See of Bath ; so
Herman had to abandon the attempt.   He is said, however,
to have built a detached bell-tower at Malmesbury.

William the Conqueror was a benefactor of the abbey, and gave it sundry valuable gifts which he had brought from his capital, Rouen, among them the head of St. Ouen, and appointed three Normans successively to rule over it. One of these, Warin de Lyrâ, annoyed that the remains of abbots of the conquered race should occupy positions of honour near the high altar, had their bodies exhumed and cast into a hole in the Chapel of St. Michael, "conglobata velut acervum ruderum." Among them was that of John the Scot, whose murder by his pupils has already been recorded. Warin, however, afterwards repented of his irreverent conduct, and in order to make some reparation he, together with Bishop Osmund of Sarum and Abbot Serlo of Gloucester, who took part in the ceremony, removed the bones of St. Ealdhelm from the stone tomb in which Dunstan had laid them, and replaced them in the original silver shrine, the gift of Ethelwulf. William's queen, Matilda, made a grant of land to the abbey, and an annual festival of five days, afterwards extended to eight, was appointed to be observed in honour of St. Ealdhelm. This festival was still observed at the time of Leland's visit in 1540.

We hear nothing of Malmesbury during the troubled days of the Red King; but important events occurred in the reign of his successor, for at that time Roger was Bishop of Sarum, and he revived the claim to the abbey that Herman had made. He was more successful than the former claimant had been, for, despite the resistance of the monks, he obtained and held the revenues for twenty years. His success was, without doubt, due to the fact that he stood high in the favour of Henry I., a much stronger king than Edward had been. Roger was a great builder. He rebuilt his own cathedral church at Old Sarum, and built castles at Sherborne, Malmesbury, and Devizes ; and he has been regarded by many authorities as the builder of the church at Malmesbury, part of which forms the church we see there at the present day. That this church was erected after his death seems certain to the writer ; but the evidence for and against the earlier date assigned by many to the building will be given. It is singularly unfortunate that we have not absolute documentary evidence of the date of this church. We would gladly give up the knowledge of the exact dates of many other dated buildings if we could only be sure of that of Malmesbury nave. A claim has been put forward that Gothic, as distinct from Romanesque, had its origin in the Ile de France, and that such Gothic features as may be met with in English work are simply importations from France, due to the buildings having been planned by or executed under the direction of French architects. Now undoubtedly the vaulting of the aisles at Malmesbury, which remains, with some trifling alterations here- after to be mentioned, just as it was left in the twelfth century, has Gothic characteristics; in this church we meet with ribbed vaulting and the pointed arch. If we could assume that these aisles were vaulted by Roger, we should be able to claim that we have a Gothic building older than St. Denis at Paris and contemporary with those earlier French churches, the ambulatory of St. Martin des Champs, Morienval, St. Etienne at Beauvais, and others, in which the Gothic principles of construction make their first appearance. And even if we must give up the date formerly confidently assumed (about 1135), we still can lay claim to the origin of Gothic in England quite apart from Ile de France influence. It seems as if when the hour for the birth of Gothic had come, the principles on which it was based appeared almost simultaneously in various districts, although when once they had been discovered there is no doubt that they were most thoroughly developed in the Ile de France.

Rickman, one of the earliest systematic writers on English architecture, gives the date of the building of Malmesbury Abbey as 1115–1139. In this he is followed by J. H. Parker. Professor Freeman gives the date of its commencement as 1135, though he allows that the nave may not have been finished until twenty or thirty years after that date; but he supposes it by no means improbable that it may have been gradually erected from one original design. Professor Moore speaks of it as nearly contemporaneous with St. Denis; that would be about 1140. Professor Moore's remarks on Malmes- bury Abbey Church are so interesting that they must be quoted in extenso :

" Few instances of the constructive use of the pointed arch, or of the employment of groin ribs in vaulting, occur in England prior to the re- building of Canterbury Cathedral by a French architect, which was begun in 1175. One instance, however, cccurs at an early date in Malmesbury

Abbey, a building which is nearly contemporaneous with St. Denis in France. Here, in the vaults of the aisles, we have a distinct approach to Gothic construction. These vaults, though simple in form and ponderous in their parts, are yet certainly advanced in character for their time. In them the principle of interpenetrating round vaults, the forms of whose

Photo.—T.P.

THE SOUTH AISLE.

arches are necessarily determined by the forms of their surfaces, gives place, in a measure, to that of an independent system of arches, which command the forms of the vaults. . . . It will be seen that the pier arch and the transverse arches are all pointed, and that the diagonals are semicircular. It will be seen, too, that the crowns of the diagonals reach to a considerably higher level than those of the transverse and longitudinal ribs, and that consequently the vaults are, like early French vaults, considerably domed. . . .

"It is evident that the central aisle was originally designed for vaulting with quadripartite vaults, since a group of three vaulting shafts rises from each pier capital. These shafts clearly belong to the original construction, as may be seen by their perfect adjustment with the imposts of the great arcade, and by their being banded by the original triforium string. They emphasise the divisions of the bays, and give a continuity to the vaulting system, like that which is characteristic of Gothic designs in France.

"The existing high vaults are of late English construction, and are ill-suited to the lower portions of the building. If the originally intended vaults were ever built over the central aisle, the effect of the interior must have been both grand and impressive, though the scale of the building is not large."—MOORE's "Development and Character of Gothic Architecture" (1890), pp. 124-126.

The advocates of the early date base their opinion on passages in the writings of William of Malmesbury, a chronicler of whom already mention has been made. So famous is this historian that a little space may be here devoted to a brief sketch of his life and writings. He was born somewhere about 1075, and since, when speaking of himself, he says "utriusque gentis sanguinem trabo," it may be inferred that he was the son of a Norman father and an English mother. He received his early education at Malmesbury Abbey, and afterwards assisted Abbot Godefrey in collecting books to form the first library of the monastery. Of this library he subsequently became librarian, and thus had ample leisure for gathering materials for his own writings. In 1140 he might have become abbot, but he declined this honourable post, probably because its duties would have given him less leisure for study. In his later days he enjoyed the friendship of Robert, Earl of Gloucester, half-brother of Matilda, and champion of her cause against Stephen. This Robert was a patron of learned men and of letters, and so was naturally attracted to the studious monk William. William, too, was a staunch supporter of Matilda, and was one of those who attended a meeting of her adherents at Winchester in 1141. Soon after this he died. His two great works are "De Gestis Regum Anglorum," which covers the ground from 449 to 1128, and is one of the chief sources of English history up to the latter date, and "De Gestis Pontificum Anglorum," which brings down the history of the church to

1140. The fifth book of this work relates the story of St. Ealdhelm, and gives far more details of it than the earlier chronicle of Faricius. We might fairly expect William to give a definite account of his own monastery, but his record is by no means so precise as we could desire. He tells us that of St. Michael's Chapel nothing more than some ruins were standing in his day. "Cujus nos vestigia vidimus." Of the Church of St. Mary, which is spoken of as Ealdhelm's, he says : "Lata majoris ecclesiæ fabrica celebris atque illibata nostro quoque perstitit ævo" ("De Gestis Pontificum," lib. v.). Professor Freeman says the use of the past tense "perstitit" clearly shows that the church was no longer standing when he wrote, and that it had been destroyed to make room for a new church during his lifetime. But "perstitit" may be translated "has stood," and is still standing as well as "stood," so that this passage does not seem conclusive evidence for the demolition of Ealdhelm's church before the time when William wrote. There is, however, a passage about Roger in the "De Gestis Regum" (lib. v.) which runs thus : "Pontifex magnanimus et nullis unquam parcens sumptibus, dum quæ facienda proponeret, ædificia præsertim, consummeret ; quod cum alias, tum maxime in Salesberia *et Malmesberia* est videre. Fecit enim ibi ædificia spatio diffusa, numero pecuniarum sumptuosa, specie formosissima ; ita juste composito ordine lapidum, ut junctura perstringat intuitum, et toto maceriam unum mentiatur esse saxum. Ecclesiam Salesberiensem et novam fecit et ornamentis excoluit, ut nulli in Anglia cedat, sed multas præcedat ; ipseque non falso possit dicere Deo 'Domine delexi decorem domus tuæ.'"

Now, with respect to this passage it may be remarked that the words *et Malmesberia* are not to be found in some texts, and, moreover, even if they are genuine, it is by no means certain that they refer to the *church* at Malmesbury, for we learn from the second book of William's "Historia Novella," a continuation of the "De Gestis Regum," that Roger had begun (*inchoaverat*) a *castle* at Malmesbury. The church at Sarum has entirely disappeared, so that we cannot compare its masonry with that of the existing church at Malmesbury, which indeed is exceedingly good, and might well be considered to accord with William's praise, when we consider that most of the buildings which he was accustomed to see had wide-jointed masonry. These passages are the only evidence that can be brought forward in favour of an earlier date than 1140 for the building or planning of the church. On the other hand, it may be said that it seems almost inconceivable that if the old church had been already pulled down, even in part, or was to be pulled down to make room for a finer church, that William, writing on the spot, should not definitely have said so, for the reconstruction of their abbey church must have been of absorbing interest to all the monks at Malmesbury living when it was in progress. The style, moreover, is decidedly advanced for the first half of the twelfth century; and it must be remembered that the Benedictines—and Malmesbury was a Benedictine house—were a very conservative body, as Mr. Prior [1] points out, and clung tenaciously to the Romanesque forms for some years after the Early English style had been employed in the churches of secular canons. Roger, indeed, may have been imbued with a love for the newer ideas, and might, if the work was his, have forced them on the monks. Still, the silence of William on the matter seems to lend weight to the opinion that nothing was actually done towards the rebuilding, even so far as the preparation of plans, before his own death. Had the choir remained to the present time, had there been any sketch or verbal description of it, the problem of the date might have been an easier one to solve. Whether the pointed arch was used in the choir we cannot tell. Beneath the central tower it certainly was not used, though there it would have been an easier expedient than the use of the stilted Norman arch, which we see on the north side, to overcome the difficulty of getting unequal spaces spanned by arches springing from the same level and rising at their crowns to the same height. This was the plan adopted in St. John's Church, Devizes, where, as at Malmesbury, the arches under the north and south sides of the tower were narrower than those beneath the east and west sides.

Another argument sometimes brought forward to show that Roger could not have built the nave of the abbey church is that he is said to have begun a castle in the very churchyard itself, not a stone's throw from the church, and that there would not have been room for the western part of the nave

[1] "History of Gothic Art in England," pp. 36, 37.

as long as the castle remained standing, and that Roger would not have planned a church part of which would occupy the site of his castle. This argument is not of much weight, as there is nothing to show that the churchyard was not at that time more extensive than now. After the dissolution of the monasteries, it is as likely that the western part of the churchyard was encroached on for building-purposes as the eastern part, where we see an Elizabethan house built upon the foundations of some of the monastic buildings. A road also has been cut through the site of the choir, and the steeple of St. Paul's Church which once stood in the churchyard is now divided from it by a road. The castle was not demolished until the time of King John, who granted to the monks its materials for building-purposes. These they may have used for some of their domestic buildings, for we have record that extensive buildings were erected during the thirteenth century, though all of these have now disappeared.

It seems reasonable to suppose that the rebuilding of the church was undertaken early in the second half of the twelfth century, possibly after the civil war was over.[1] As the country round the abbey was in a disturbed condition during the reign of Stephen, much of the fighting taking place in the neighbourhood, it seems hardly likely that this time would have been chosen by the monks for extensive building-operations. The character of the architecture itself would indicate the second half of the twelfth century as the most probable time for the erection of the church. The massive pillars of the nave, the round-headed arches, and the chevron moulding of the triforium are remnants of the Norman style, while the pointed arches of the nave arcading are an early introduction of the style which was destined to prevail in the thirteenth century. It may be noticed that the pointed arches are not very sharp,[2] and that, as at Wimborne Minster, their pointed character is somewhat masked by the grotesque heads carved at their points. It is also worthy of note that pointed arches are only found in connection with the vaulting of the aisles—namely, in the main arcading of the nave and the transverse arches of the aisle vaulting. In the triforium both

[1] The compact between Stephen and Henry which ended the war was made at Malmesbury in 1153.

[2] They meet on an angle of about 150°.

the main and sub arches are Norman in character. The clerestory was from the first very fully developed, as can be seen from the exterior pilasters, which rise almost to the top of the walls; this shows that the walls were not much raised when the clerestory was reconstructed in the fourteenth century, and the church covered, probably for the first time, with stone vaulting. It is evident that a stone vault was contemplated from the first, although for a time probably the nave was covered by a wooden ceiling. The original clerestory was without doubt pierced by tall, narrow, round-headed windows. The central tower was probably originally a lantern, such as that at Wells and Salisbury, though, like them, it afterwards had a vault inserted beneath it. This was done at Malmesbury during the Perpendicular period, possibly with a view of making the church warmer and more comfortable for the monks, as some of the choir-stalls were situated beneath the tower.

ELEVATION OF A BAY OF THE NAVE
(From Britton's English Architecture.)

Although we cannot exactly date the rebuilding of Malmesbury Abbey Church, we may safely say that it is a very early
example of Transitional work.   The treatment of the pointed
arch in the groining is more systematic than that of the pointed
arches in the vaulting of the nave at Durham, which is dated
1128–1133, and is earlier than the Transitional work at
Kirkstall, which was completed in 1182, and the Transitional
work at Wells in Bishop Reginald's time.   Thus the church at
Malmesbury forms an important link in the chain connecting
the Romanesque and Gothic.

In 1190 a dispute again arose between the monks and the
new Bishop of Sarum, Hubert Walter, who had been consecrated in 1189.   The story shall be given in the quaint
words of the chronicler, Richard of Devizes : "The King of
Darkness that ancient firebrand between the church of Sarum
and the Abbey of Malmesbury applying fresh fuel kindled the
old fire into a blaze.   The Abbot was summoned not upon
the question of making his profession to the Bishop, but that
of laying aside altogether his name and the staff of a pastor.
The King's [1] letter to the Chancellor was produced, ordering
the Abbot to answer in law to the demands of the Bishop of
Sarum.   But the Abbot (Robert de Melun), whose fortune was
at stake, was one whom no danger found unprepared, and who
was not a man to lose anything by cowardice.   He gave blow
for blow, and got other letters from the King counteracting the
former ones.   The Chancellor, perceiving the shameful con-
tradictions in the King's mandates, in order that the King's
character might not suffer if any further steps were taken, put
the whole case off until the King's return "; and then the
whole matter seems to have dropped.

King John proved himself a benefactor to the abbey, and,
as has been stated above, gave the monks the materials of the
castle built by Bishop Roger, and, moreover, in the seventeenth
year of his reign, bestowed on them the Manor of Malmesbury.

The most casual examination of the church will show that
there is no thirteenth-century or Early English work to be seen
in it.   There seems a gap in its architectural history of a
whole century.   Much twelfth-century work, as we have seen,
there is ; fourteenth- and fifteenth-century work may also be

[1] Richard I., who had gone to the crusade, leaving Longchamp, Bishop
of Ely, Chancellor of the Realm and Governor in his stead.

seen. What were the monks about during that great building-epoch, when the Cistercians were so busy in Yorkshire, when the great secular Church of Lincoln received its most splendid additions, and St. Mary's rose on a new foundation at Salisbury? It seems probable that, the church having been completed and standing in all its massive grandeur, the abbot and monks rested for a time contented with the work, and then, when once again they turned their attention to architectural work in the second half of the thirteenth century, it was not upon the church, but upon the domestic buildings that they spent their money and their labour. It was by William de

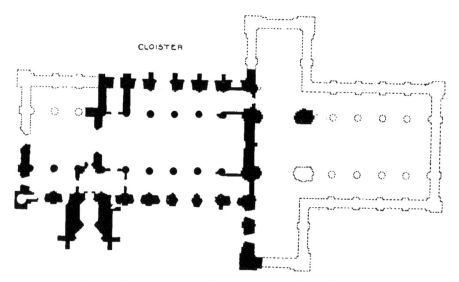

CLOISTER

RESTORED GROUND PLAN OF MALMESBURY ABBEY.

Colerne, who became abbot in 1260, that the great work of remodelling and rebuilding the various parts of the abbey were directed. We hear of a great hall and a lesser hall, of a kitchen and a larder, of a dormitory and a chapter-house, of a bakehouse and a brewhouse, of a stable and a workshop, all built or rebuilt by him; we also read of his planting a vineyard and enclosing it with a stone wall, and of his making a garden of herbs adjoining it and of his planting vines and apple-trees in his own garden. Moreover, he improved the water supply, and the stream he led into the abbey by a conduit flowed into the lavatory for the first time on St. Martin's Day, 1284.

All these buildings have vanished, destroyed after the dissolution; in them, had they remained, we should have found examples of the Early English style.

About the same time a hospital of the Order of St. John of Jerusalem was founded at Malmesbury near the south bridge. A single arch of this is still standing. In the thirteenth century we find mention of the Church of St. Paul, the vicar of which was appointed and paid by the abbey. This no doubt stood on the same site as the Church of St. Paul, all of which has been swept away save the steeple, which now serves as a bell-tower for the present parish church.

We have little written record of Malmesbury Abbey for many years, but from studying the building we can discover what was being done during the fourteenth and fifteenth centuries. No eastern extension seems to have been made after the church was finished in the twelfth century, unless it were the lady-chapel mentioned by William of Worcester, who visited Malmesbury in the time of Henry V. He tells us he measured its length and breadth, as he did the other dimensions of the church, not by any measuring-rod, but by counting his own steps. We are informed in Dugdale's " New Monasticon " that William of Worcester's step was $19\frac{1}{2}$ in. This value seems rather too small, for there are some parts of the building which we can still measure whose length William of Worcester gives in his own steps. The interior projection of the transepts beyond the aisles is 39 ft. William of Worcester says the projection of the transepts beyond the aisles is 22 steps, but he does not say whether he is speaking of interior projection or not. If he is, then his step must have been about 21 in. The lady-chapel, he says, measured 36 of his steps in length and 9 in breadth, which would make it about $58\frac{1}{2}$ by $14\frac{1}{2}$ ft., or 63 by 15 ft. 9 in., according to the value we give his step—$19\frac{1}{2}$ or 21 in. This is exceedingly narrow if the length of the chapel ran east and west; but it may have run across the east end of the choir. He gives as the total length of the building 172 steps—that is, about 280 or 300 ft.

A considerable amount of work was done during the fourteenth century. The clerestory was remodelled and larger windows inserted in it. The walls of the eastern part are probably the original twelfth-century walls; but the western parts have been rebuilt. The present vaulting was thrown over the nave, and flying buttresses and pinnacles were added to counteract the weight of the new roof. Besides these changes, two large windows with very peculiar tracery were inserted in the south aisle and one in the north aisle. The sills of the other windows were brought lower down. These alterations were no doubt made partly to admit more light (for mediæval Churchmen had no predilection for "a dim religious light"), partly to display painted glass. The peculiar tracery of the windows on the south side (see illustration, p. 74) may have been designed with reference to the subjects of the glass that was destined to fill them. On the north side, as the cloister would not allow of the sill of the new window being brought down so low as those on the south side, a gable was carried up in the aisle wall, and vaulting introduced below it. In the fourteenth century also the south porch was cased on its southern side, the old hood moulding and terminations being either copied or used again. It is almost certain that the porch never received a vault, for, if it had, there would have been no occasion for placing the present ceiling below it. A parapet was also added to the walls of the nave, the aisle, and porch on the south side, but not on the north.

At what time the central tower, which probably at first did not rise much above the ridge of the roof, was raised and the spire added we cannot tell. The spire, which is said to have been more lofty than that of the cathedral church at Salisbury, probably consisted of a timber framework covered with lead.

In the fifteenth century a western tower was built. It may be that the addition of a spire and the tampering with the arches beneath the central tower when the vaulting was introduced beneath the lantern had rendered it risky to ring the ten bells which hung in the central tower, so that another tower was built to contain them. But this western tower was built in a most insecure way. It was not erected upon foundations on the ground beyond the west front, but its western face was built upon the existing west wall of the church, the north and south faces on the clerestory walls, and the eastern face upon an arch crossing above the vaulting of the nave but below the external roof. To strengthen it an additional flying buttress was inserted on the south side beneath the fourteenth-century flying buttress; of this we may be sure, since it has remained to our own day, although it has been rebuilt during the restoration commenced at the end of the last century. Probably a similar buttress was built at the north side also. A flying buttress was also built eastward across the clerestory window, which may still be seen on the south side.

At the same time a large Perpendicular window was inserted in the west front, and a Perpendicular doorway within the original great western doorway, which was partially walled up. Whether this was done to strengthen the wall or simply for æsthetic reasons we cannot tell. Both the towers fell—we do not know exactly when; all we know is that Leland, writing in 1540, says the church had two steeples: "one that had a mightie high pyramis felle daungerously in hominum memoriâ and sins was not re-edified, it stode on the middle of the transeptum of the church and was a marke to al the countrie aboute. The other yet stondeth, a great square toure at the west end of the chierch." The ruin, however, of the central tower was not so complete as it is now, for it is recorded that portions of its pillars were thrown down by the concussion of guns fired to celebrate the Restoration of Charles II. The rood-screen beneath the western arch of the central tower was not destroyed, but still stands as a reredos to the present church. The carving on this, however, indicates a date late in the fifteenth century.

Professor Freeman thinks that before the central tower actually fell the monks having abandoned the choir and crossing migrated into the nave for safety, for he says: "Just east of the rood-screen the arch is built up as high as the impost with a solid wall which appears to be older than the destruction of the eastern part of the church. I ground this belief chiefly on the fact that the masonry up to this height is quite different and of a much better character than that which blocks the arch itself, which last exactly resembles that with which the arches between the transepts and the nave aisles were clearly blocked at the time of the destruction." He is inclined to believe that when the tower showed signs of weakness the wall upon the rood-screen was introduced to remedy the weakness and put off the evil day for a time.

During the fifteenth century Perpendicular tracery was inserted in the Norman windows of the aisles, and the cloister door was reduced in size.

The string course above the nave arcading seems, for some

unaccountable reason, to have been partially hacked away
some time before the fall of the western tower, for we find
that the string course above the arcading of the ruined part
of the church was treated in the same way.

The watching-loft projecting from the south triforium is of
late fourteenth or early fifteenth-century date.

Photo.—T.F.

THE WATCHING LOFT.

We cannot fix the date of the fall of the western tower
within very close limits. All we know is, that it was standing
at the time of Leland's visit (1540), but that it was gone in
1634, for a tourist, whose name we do not know, visited
the church in that year, and says he found the two turrets
at the west end quite demolished, but says nothing of any
western tower. He apparently had no knowledge that such

a tower ever existed. It would therefore appear that in all probability the fall was not a recent event in 1634. At some time after the tower fell the present west wall of the church was built, cutting off the two western bays of the nave, and a finely proportioned window was inserted in it. The tracery of this is modern. The vaulting of the two western bays within the existing church, as well as that of the two still farther to the west, was ruined by the fall of the tower. The stone vault was never replaced, but within the present church a very well-executed plaster vault was put up to take its place.

In the time of Edward III. the Abbot of Malmesbury was, with twenty-four other abbots, summoned to sit in Parliament; but it was not until the days of Richard II. that the abbot received a mitre.

In the reign of Henry VIII. the abbey was dissolved. The exact date of the surrender was December 15, 1539. The last abbot, Selwyn, together with about twenty monks, were pensioned off, and all the abbey property was seized by the king. The annual value was returned to the king's commissioners as £803.

After the dissolution the monastic buildings gradually disappeared. Some portions were seen by the anonymous tourist above mentioned in 1634, and John Aubrey in 1650 speaks of the remains of the kitchen standing on four strong pillars to the north-west of the church.

The Tudor house, still known as Abbey House, to the north-east, was built upon the lower story of some part of the domestic buildings, possibly the infirmary. The original windows may still be seen on the north side. Once there was a central row of pillars within the undercroft, but these have now been destroyed, together with the vaulting, and the undercroft is used as a wine-cellar. It is supposed by some that the house above this was built by William Stump, a rich clothier of North Nibley, in Gloucestershire, who for the sum of £1,500 bought of Henry VIII. the site of the abbey and the buildings thereon standing. He used some of the domestic buildings as workshops, others as residences for his workmen, filling even the chapel at the south end of the transept with looms, but presented the remains of the nave to the parish, to be used as a parish church in place of the dilapidated church of St. Paul.

The tower of this church and its spire, a broach of the Perpendicular period, alone remain to the present day, and serve as a campanile for St. Mary's, which has no bells of its own, seeing that no tower remains in which bells could be hung. Before the fall of the central tower it contained ten bells, one of which bore the name of St. Ealdhelm, and was rung to scare away lightning.

It was on August 20, 1541, that Cranmer granted the license for the use of the nave of the parish church for parochial purposes.

At the time of the dissolution the manuscripts of the abbey library were scattered—some were sold as wastepaper or parchment; some, says John Aubrey, were used by him and his schoolfellows to cover their school-books; he also tells us that Mr. William Stump, great-grandson of the purchaser of the abbey, had several of the abbey manuscripts. " He was a proper man and a good fellow ; and when he brewed a barrel of special ale his use was to stop the bung-hole, under the clay, with a sheet of manuscript ; he said nothing did it so well, which methought did grieve me much to see. Afterwards I went to school to Mr. Latimer at Leigh Delamere, where was the like use of covering of books. In my grand father's days the manuscripts flew about like butterflies. All music books, account books, copy books &c were covered with old manuscripts as we cover them now with blue or marbled paper : and the glovers of Malmesbury made great havoc of them and gloves were wrapped up in many good pieces of antiquity." When he was grown up Aubrey went to his first school at Yatton-Keynell. to see if he could find any remains of Parson Stump's manuscripts, but he could light on none. " His sons were gunners and soldiers and had scoured their guns with them "; but he saw some ancient deeds bearing the abbey seal. Some few scraps of Malmesbury manuscripts were discovered, though in a very mutilated condition, by the late Rev. Canon Jackson, for many years rector of Leigh Delamere, the parish of which Latimer, Aubrey's schoolmaster, was rector in the seventeenth century. These manuscripts were shown by Canon Jackson at a meeting of the Wilts Archæological Society at Malmesbury, and, despite the rough usage to which they had been subjected, still showed traces of gold lettering and the beautiful penmanship of the monks,

THE SOUTH-WEST ANGLE.

After the destruction of the cloister of the abbey, buttresses were built against the walls of the north aisle.

Malmesbury, during the civil war of the seventeenth century, was alternately occupied by Roundheads and Cavaliers, for it lay on the direct road between Bristol and Oxford, the respective headquarters of the opposite parties during a considerable part of the war. What injury, if any, was done to the church during this period we do not know, though during the Commonwealth it was not used for divine worship.

At the present time extensive works of repair and restoration are in progress. This work will not probably be completed for some time. The condition of the fabric was such that immediate steps were needed to secure it from further ruin. The restoration of an old building is always a process fraught with danger: incumbents often wish to make their churches smart ; architects, builders, and masons always want to do too much and to insert modern imitations of old work. There is some hope, however, that at Malmesbury less mischief than usual will be done, and that the church, when it emerges from the restorers' hands, will be not a practically new building, but an old one repaired and made sound throughout, yet still retaining its old features. Some objection may, however, be fairly made to the new carved finials placed on the pinnacles on the south side, which might better have been left in their truncated condition. The writer has had the opportunity of examining the report prepared jointly by the Society of Antiquaries and the Society for the Protection of Ancient Buildings. This report contains some admirable suggestions for the extension of the church westward. It is recommended that the two ruined bays at the west end should be rebuilt and this part of the church covered with a timber roof, but that the north aisle should not be extended farther to the west, as it would be unwise to tamper with the solid buttresses; that the present west wall should be retained, with its window and tracery left intact, though the glass might be removed from it. If an arch were built beneath the window to support the weight of the west wall, the modern organ-gallery, with the round-headed arches of modern date on which it stands, might be removed so as to give a greater appearance of length. The rebuilt western portion of the church would form a kind of vestibule to the church if an entrance were made in the new west wall, which should be built without interfering in any way with the remains of the original doorway. The whole scheme would be somewhat costly, and it is doubtful if funds will allow of its being carried out for some time to come.

Photo.—T.F

MARKET CROSS.

The present contract provides for the rebuilding of the western part of the nave arcade on the south side only, with the triforium and clerestory above it, the roofing of the ruined part of the south aisle, the demolition of the walls across this aisle just to the east of the porch, and the removal further to the west of the wall which forms the present west end of the aisle, so as to throw the whole aisle open from east to west, and the building of a temporary wall under the renewed arches of the nave arcading, so as to enclose the aisle on its north side.

Before leaving the history of the building it may be well to briefly notice the fine market-cross standing outside the present churchyard to the south. Leland speaks of it having been built *hominum memoriâ*; this well accords with its architectural features, which indicate a fifteenth-century date. It is octagonal; a groined roof springs from a central pier. In character it much resembles the Poultry Cross at Salisbury and the cross at Chichester. The gateway leading into the present churchyard at the south-east is much more modern in construction, though some of the stonework seems old; it was probably erected in the seventeenth century.

THE SOUTH SIDE FROM THE PORCH ROOF.

REMAINS OF THE WEST FRONT.

CHAPTER II.

THE EXTERIOR.

THE church at Malmesbury as we see it to-day, like those at Pershore and Hexham, is but a fragment of the old abbey church, and in some respects has fared worse than these two churches, for while they can each boast of the possession of a tower, and the former of one wing of the transept, and the latter of the whole transept, Malmesbury has lost both its towers and transepts, is ruinous at both ends, and the church, as used for service at the present day, consists of little more than the six eastern bays of the original nave, its two aisles, and the great southern porch. Outside the part now roofed in, the arch, above which once rose the north wall of the central tower, still stands in all its lofty ruined grandeur, as also do the west wall and south-west angle of the south transept, and the south aisle wall to the west of the porch, a portion

of the clerestory at this part of the church, and the southern
half of the west front, but all in a more or less ruined
condition.

It will be convenient to begin the examination of the exterior of the building with the remains of the **west front**.
The south jamb of the original great west door may still
be seen, and enough of the mouldings of the arch remains
to show that the carving was of an elaborate character. On
one order were represented the signs of the Zodiac, of which
three only remain, in an almost unrecognisable state. There
never was more than one entrance to the church at the west
end; there are no doorways giving admission to the aisles.
Above the west doorway there was once a great window—a
Perpendicular insertion in the Norman walls, as we infer
from the remains of the ends of the four transoms by which
it was divided. To the south of the doorway may be seen
some intersecting arches of the arcading, which, interrupted
here and there, runs along the west front and the south
side of the church and along that part of the transept that
still remains.

The west end beyond the central part, which no doubt,
before the erection of the western tower, terminated in a
gable, is a simple screen of stone-work running out to a turret,
oblong in plan, at the south-west angle. Malmesbury, therefore,
like Salisbury and Exeter and other churches, had a western
façade bearing no relation to the nave and aisles that it
terminated. Professor Freeman remarks that nowhere else
in English Romanesque has he found a similar sham wall.
Above the arcading just mentioned, in this part cut into to
allow of the insertion of a rectangular tablet, is a richly
ornamented window with chevron moulding and semicircular
drip-stone, with the remains of inserted Perpendicular tracery,
and above it a string course which runs round the buttresses and
turret. Above this is an arcade of two complete arches, with
half arches on either side with richly carved mouldings
without capitals. Underneath each of the two central arches
of this arcade are two sub-arches rising from shafts with
capitals; above this is another string course, and then another
row of arcading consisting of five semicircular, non-intersecting
arches with plain mouldings underneath a plain string course,
and then a plain wall, once probably terminating in a parapet,

which has, however, disappeared. Of the south-west turret three complete stages and a portion of the fourth still stand; the lowest is plain, with no openings. On the western and southern faces of the second are two lofty semicircular-headed arches. Beneath the two on the western face are other semi-circular-headed arches. The wall beneath the eastern arch on the south side is pierced by a long slit; over the second stage is an ornamental string course, above which the turret recedes; the next stage is decorated on the south and west

faces with an arcade of intersecting semicircular arches springing from shafts with capitals. The fourth stage, of which only the lower part re-mains, is decorated with ·richly carved pilasters; similar pilasters are to be seen also on the eastern face, the corners being occupied by carved cylindrical shafts.

Turning round the angle, we find between the south-western turret and the south porch two bays of the aisle wall with a flat buttress be-tween them. Along the wall of the western bay the arcade of intersect-

Photo.—T.P.

THE SOUTH-WEST TURRET.

ing arches is resumed, but it is not seen in the next bay. Each bay contains a round-headed window with inserted Perpendicular tracery, but without glass. In fact, the whole of the western part of the building consists of walls without a roof; hence, of course, no glass is found in the windows. Against the wall, between the first and second windows of the clerestory, count-ing from the west before the restoration was begun, rested two flying buttresses, one above the other, a second one having become necessary to support the extra weight when the western tower was built. This part of the wall is, at the time of writing, being rebuilt; the flying buttresses and the lofty pinnacles against which they abut have been one by one rebuilt of the old stones as far as possible, and at the same time fresh tracery and glass have been inserted in the clerestory windows. It is said that this part of the church was in such an unsafe condition that the parishioners were afraid to sit in the nave whenever a strong south wind was blowing, lest the clerestory windows should be blown in and fall on the heads of those seated below.

We next come to the great glory of the church, of which the people of Malmesbury are so justly proud—the magnificent

CARVING ON THE SOUTH PORCH.

south porch. This projects a considerable distance from the aisle wall, and may be divided into three parts: the outer casing and buttresses, added in the fourteenth century; the twelfth-century arch; and the side-walls and inner doorway. The outer facing has plain mouldings encircled by a hood moulding terminating in monsters' heads of the same form as may be seen at the extremities of the hood-moulding over the arches of the nave arcading. Just within this is a plain arch, and then the original outer porch recessed in eight orders. These run round the porch without any capitals, and are profusely decorated with sculpture. The first, third, fifth, seventh, and eighth of these orders, counting inwards, are carved with scroll-work; the second, fourth, and sixth are carved with figure subjects set in ovals of scroll-work; but unfortunately they are so much weathered that many of them can now with difficulty, if at all, be made out. The process of decay has been very rapid in recent times. *The Builder*, in the number for March 2, 1895, contains a reproduction of an old engraving by Le Keux, by comparing which with recent photographs it may be seen how much the carving has been weathered in recent years.[1] The anonymous tourist who visited the church in 1634, and has left an account of the then

Photo.—T.P.

THE. SOUTH PORCH.

[1] When I was at the church in November, 1900, the daughter of a former vicar, who also happened to be visiting the church, remarked on the great advance of decay that had taken place since her father's death.

existing condition of the abbey church in his "Topographical Excursion," printed in *Brayley's Graphic and Historical Illustrator*, p. 411, gives a minute description of the sculpture on the porch. Beginning at the bottom of each arch on the western side, he enumerates the subjects thus :

FIRST OR INNER ARCH.   SECOND OR MIDDLE.   THIRD OR OUTER.

1. Defaced quite.
2. Light from chaos.

1.⎫ God sits and be-
2.⎭ holds the sins of the world.

1.⎫ Defaced quite.
2.⎭

3. The sea from the land.

3. Cain a fugitive.

3. John, the forerunner of Christ.

4. The Lord sits and beholds.

4. He comes to Eve.

4. Michael the Archangel.

5. He makes fowls.

5. An angel.

5. The angels come to Mary.

6. He makes fish.

6. God delivers Noah the axe.

6. Mary in child-bed.

7. He makes the beasts.

7. Noah works on the ark.

7. The three wise men come to Christ.

8. The spirit moving on the waters.

8. Eight persons saved.

8. They find Him.

9. Adam made.

9. Abraham offers Isaac.

9. Joseph, Mary, and Christ go into Egypt.

10. Adam sleeps and woman made.

10. The lamb caught in the bush.

10. Christ curses the fig-tree.

11. Paradise.

11. Moses talks with his father.

11. He rides on an ass to Jerusalem.

12. Adam left there.

12. Moses keeping sheep.

12. He eats the Passover with His twelve Apostles.

13. Devil tempts Eve.

13. Moses and Aaron striking the rock.

13. He is nailed to the cross.

14. They hide themselves.

14. Moses reads the Law to the elders.

14. Laid in the tomb by Joseph.

15. God calls to them.

15 Samson tearing the lion.

15. He riseth again.

16. God thrusts them out.

16. Samson bearing the city gates.

16. He ascendeth into heaven.

17. A spade and distaff given.

17. The Philistines put out his eyes.

17. The Holy Ghost descending on the Apostles.

18. Adam digs, Eve spins.

18. David rescues the lamb,

18. Michael overthrows the devil,

FIRST OR INNER ARCH.	SECOND OR MIDDLE.	THIRD OR OUTER.
19. Eve brings forth Cain.	19. David fights with Goliath.	19. Mary mourning for Jesus.
20. Abel tills the earth.	20. Goliath slain.	20.⎫
21.⎱ Two angels for	21. An angel.	21.⎬ Demolished quite.
22.⎰ keepers.	22. David rests himself.	22.⎪
23. Abel walks in the fields.	23. Defaced quite.	23.⎭
24. Cain meets him.	24. David walks to Beth-boron.	
25. Cain kills Abel.	25. David's entertainment there.	
26.⎫	26.⎫	
27.⎬ Demolished quite.	27.⎭ Demolished quite.	
28.⎭		

Professor Cockerell, in his work on the sculpture on the west front of Wells, also gives his reading of the Malmesbury sculptures. He agrees with the tourist with respect to Nos. 9, 10, 11, 13, 14, 15, 16, 17, and 25 on the first arch; No. 23 he takes to represent Abel's sacrifice. He agrees with the list of subjects given above for Nos. 6, 7, 8, 9, 10, 13, 15, 16, 18, and 19 on the middle arch; but thinks No. 1 represents God's command to Noah, No. 11 the burning bush, No. 14 the rod of Moses. Speaking of the outer arch, he commences with No. 5, and generally agrees, save that he omits No. 17, and for No. 10 gives Christ before the doctors, and the betrayal.

Within the outer archway is the inner porch, rectangular in plan, with bench tables on either side, above each of which is an arcade of four arches, round-headed, with chevron moulding springing from capitals with square abaci, themselves richly carved; but all the shafts, save the end ones, have disappeared. Above the arcading on either side, under a semicircular arch, is a group of six seated figures with angels flying above them, all in high relief. The seated figures probably represent the twelve apostles. These carvings seem of earlier date than those on the outer arches, and may have belonged to the earlier Church of St. Mary existing in William of Malmesbury's day. The doorway leading into the church is recessed in three orders, elaborately carved with scroll patterns. The tympanum over the door contains a carving of Christ and attendant angels. A holy-water stoup stands on the east side of the door. The ceiling of the porch is a plain tunnel roof of plaster. The floor is paved with rough flagstones much worn. Before the restoration is completed a new pavement will probably be laid ; it is to be hoped that it will be of stone, not of tiles, which would not harmonise with the old stone-work.

Above the porch, as is so often the case, is a chamber, lighted here by a two-light rectangular window with square, leaded panes. The porch has buttresses at the corners, set at right angles to its faces ; it is finished at the top by a horizontal pierced parapet, behind which the lead roof rises to a very

TYMPANUM OF THE SOUTH DOORWAY.

obtuse angle ; from the base of the parapet the heads of two monsters project. The outer porch is protected by some ugly iron railings with gates running between the two buttresses that project from the southern face of the porch. These are to be removed, so that the recessed entrance will be much better seen.

In the angle between the east side of the porch and the wall of the aisle is a rectangular turret rising just above the wall of the nave, with a pyramidal roof, covered, as the roof of the aisles are, with stone shingles ; this contains a newel staircase leading up to the chamber above the porch, and also to the triforium on the south side. Access to this staircase can be gained either from the exterior or interior of the church.

To the east of the porch there are five bays, divided along the **south aisle** wall by flat pilasters ; in the first two are round-headed windows with inserted Perpendicular tracery, and beneath them an arcading of intersecting arches rising from square capitals ; the next two bays contain large Decorated windows deeply splayed. To make room for these, since their sills are much nearer to the ground than those of the windows whose place they took, the arcading was cut away and a plain wall built. The fifth bay is similar to the first and second, and here the original arcading remains. The windows of the clerestory contain Decorated tracery, and all save the eastern-most one have three lights ; this last is narrower and has only two lights. The parapets that run along the top of the walls of the aisles and clerestory are similar to the one that runs round the walls of the porch. A very fine series of flying buttresses was added to support the thrust of the stone vault when the clerestory was remodelled and the nave vaulted with the existing roof in the fourteenth century (see p. 64).

The walls surrounding the three easternmost windows of the clerestory are ornamented with projecting carved medal-lions ; there are five on each side of the window nearest the transept, and three on each side of the other two win-dows. One of these medallions is modern, and, according to the principle wisely adopted in the restoration, it is left quite plain. Wherever new work is added, as in the case of a pillar which was built to take the place of one that had fallen, the mouldings are left perfectly plain, so that for all succeeding time a distinction may be seen between the old and the modern work. This principle, however, has not been adopted in the new stone-work introduced into the tracery of the clerestory windows. The original flat buttresses may be seen running up against the eastern half of the clerestory wall, but there are no such buttresses against the western half of the wall, which probably was rebuilt in the fourteenth century. The wall that rises at the east end above the roof of the aisle is provided with an external flight of steps leading up to the roof of the nave from the ruined west wall of the transept. These steps have been renewed, but an old print represents such a stairway existing before the recent work of

DECORATED WINDOWS, SOUTH SIDE. *Photo.—T.P.*

restoration.   The flying buttresses rest on vertical buttresses
rising within the parapet, with gabled heads, and loaded with

plain, massive, and lofty pinnacles rising to about the level of the parapet of the clerestory, the easternmost pinnacle alone being lower. The pyramidal part of these pinnacles rises from within a battlement that runs round their bases. These have been rebuilt, and the finials are new.

The **transept** never had any aisle on the west side, nor can traces of any aisle having ever existed on the east side be found; possibly, however, there may have been one or more apsidal chapels. The west wall of the south transept is still standing. It consists of two bays divided by a flat buttress; at its base runs arcading similar to that which is seen along the wall of the south aisle; above it in each bay is a Norman window, in which there are no signs of inserted tracery; and again, immediately above a string course, which runs on the same level as the parapet of the aisle wall in each bay may be seen another Norman window. In the thickness of the wall at this level a gallery is pierced, which probably communicated with the triforium of the nave. When we get round the end of the wall, and are able to examine the other side, which was, of course, originally the interior wall of the transept, we find some traces of an arcading of non-intersecting arches under a carved string course. The lower windows above this are deeply splayed, and on either side of each of the upper windows are narrow, round-headed, arched openings communicating with the passage mentioned above; but these are not symmetrically placed. The character of this wall will be better understood from an examination of the accompanying illustration than from any verbal description. At the south end of the transept wall may be seen traces of weather moulding. This may indicate that a chapel once projected farther southward; indeed, it is quite possible that this was the site of the small church spoken of in the records of the abbey, which, after the dissolution, Leland says he saw filled with weavers' looms.

The pointed arch which once led from the south aisle into the transept still remains, but it has been walled up; and above it may be seen the wide, round-headed archway opening out from the triforium, which has been blocked by masonry, through which a small rectangular opening has been made to give light to the triforium.

The great western arch between the crossing and the nave

THE RUINED TOWER AND PRESENT EAST END.

has been blocked with a wall that forms the east end of the present church. The arch is semicircular. Above it may be seen portions of the ribs of the vaulting which was inserted below the lantern. Three of the piers that supported the central tower remain, the south-east pier alone having dis-appeared. The tower arch piers consist of clustered shafts with square abaci. The tower itself was square in plan, but, probably with a view of providing as much blank wall as possible behind the choir-stalls, the piers are longer in section from east to west than from north to south, and the existing arch on the north side is seen to be much narrower in span than the west arch. It is consequently considerably stilted. Above this arch the vaulting ribs may be seen in a more perfect condition than over the west arch of the tower; the ribs meet in a boss of carved foliage. A fragment of the choir arcading still remains. The lower part of the arch springing from clustered shafts may be seen, and above it the shafts and a small piece of the chevron moulding of the westernmost arch of the triforium of the choir. The eastern end of the north aisle of the nave has been blocked up, and a small doorway inserted beneath the arch.

The exterior walls of the **north side** of the nave and its aisle are much plainer than the corresponding walls on the south side of the church. It was on this side that the cloister was built. Though monks generally preferred the south side of the nave for the cloister garth and its surrounding walks, and naturally so, since they got the advantage of the sun to warm and light three out of the four walks in which so much of their time was passed, yet occasionally the character of the ground induced them to depart from the usual custom, as they did at Malmesbury and in the not far distant Benedictine Abbey Church of St. Peter at Gloucester. The entrance to the church from the domestic buildings of the abbey was along the east walk of the cloister, through a lofty Norman doorway which led into the north aisle. This doorway may still be seen; but at some time during the Perpendicular era it was walled up and a smaller doorway made through the inserted masonry. This opening was not cut centrally, but is nearer to the east side. Some traces of the moulding of the depressed arch still remains, but it no longer opens into the aisle, as a thin wall has been built within it, its inner side flush with the interior wall, so that only a recess in the great thickness of the Norman wall remains on the outside.   There is no arcading along the wall of the north aisle of the nave, but above the second offset of the buttresses[1] there is a row of windows, one in each bay.   With the exception of one to be mentioned immediately, they are of Norman date, and have had Perpendicular tracery inserted. In the fourth bay from the east a large Decorated window has been inserted, and to allow sufficient space for this the wall has been raised into a gable, forming a very pleasing feature on this side of the church.   It will be remembered that two windows of a somewhat similar character are to be seen on the south side of the church ; but then, as the sills could be brought near to the ground, there was no reason for raising the wall to accommodate their heads.   Here, however, the cloister compelled the builder to keep the bottom of the window at a considerable height, so that he had to raise the wall to get room for the top of the window.   Whether it was ever intended to alter all the windows in like manner we cannot tell.   Doubtless the desire to obtain more light and to have the opportunity of displaying painted glass led to the change being made some time during the fourteenth century ; possibly lack of funds—for the abbey was not one of the richest—led to the change not being carried out more fully.   The Abbot of Malmesbury once had a great opportunity, which would have led to the enriching of his abbey, presented to him, but he was not brave enough to accept the chance; for when a last resting-place for the body of King Edward II., murdered at Berkeley Castle, was requested of Adam, Abbot of Malmesbury, he, like the Abbots of Bristol and Kingswood, refused to give his permission for the burial, and it was left to brave Thokey, Abbot of the Benedictine house of Gloucester, to receive the body within his walls.   Had Abbot Adam granted the request, the money which in after years poured into the coffers of Gloucester from the hands of pilgrims who visited the tomb of Edward would have increased the revenues of Malmesbury, with the result that this most interesting church—the best specimen on a large scale that we possess of the transition from Romanesque to Gothic—would in all probability have been altogether rebuilt,

---

[1] The lower parts of the buttresses beneath the level of the window-sills are comparatively modern, and did not project, as they now do, while the cloister existed.

or at any rate so much altered that its chief interest would have been destroyed; hence we may well feel thankful for the caution shown by the abbot, though no doubt his successors often regretted that he had let the chance of enriching their house pass away unused.

In the last bay that still remains on this side of the church there is a doorway with an elliptic head. The flying buttresses on this side resemble those on the south side of the church, but the pinnacles are not finished with carved finials. In place also of flying buttresses two massive, solid buttresses, or rather walls, flank each side of the bay nearest the west. These descend through the roof of the aisle down to the floor and, as we shall find when examining the interior of the church, form a small chamber at the west end of the north aisle. These walls were probably built after the fall of the western tower to secure the church from further injury. The tower would seem to have fallen chiefly towards the north. This was fortunate; otherwise, the great south porch might have been crushed. The three western bays of the north aisle were destroyed, together with the adjoining arcading of the nave, and the vault over the five western bays of the nave, and the vault over the two western bays of the south aisle. The two easternmost nave bays of the part of the church damaged by the fall were repaired, and a wall was built to the west of these to form the west end of the church. In this wall was inserted a lofty, well-proportioned window. Its tracery, of flowing Decorated type, is a modern restoration.

To the west of the outside of this wall the original church extended rather more than two and a half bays. Three pillars may be seen on the south side. The first is original, but is partially embedded in the walls erected after the fall of the tower to form a kind of lobby to the north of the great porch. The third is really a respond attached to the original west wall of the church. The second has been recently rebuilt. These piers are of the same character as those of the nave arcading to be described in the next chapter, with huge cylindrical shafts and circular abaci with scalloped capitals beneath, with the exception of the one that has been rebuilt, whose capital has purposely been left plain to show that it is modern work.

The whole of the exterior of what still remains of the abbey church has now been described in sufficient detail. The

mutilated condition detracts considerably from its appearance
as a whole.   But in the state in which it existed after the
erection of the western tower, and before the fall of the
central spire, and with all its domestic buildings standing—that
is to say, during the second half of the fifteenth century—it
must have been one of the most imposing of English abbeys.
The site alone would give it a dignity that many other similar
buildings never possessed.   Durham and Lincoln only could
boast of sites as good.
The abbey buildings
stood on a lofty plateau
flanked by a steep
escarpment on the
northern side.   The
abrupt nature of this
escarpment is best seen
from the railway just
before it enters the
station, or from the foot-
path running up from
the station by the side
of the little stream
called Newnton Water,
on which once stood
the abbey mill, and on
which its successor still
stands to the north side
of the abbey grounds.
Let us, as we stand at
the foot of this hill, rebuild in imagination the
square western tower
flanked by its two tur-

THE PRESENT WEST WINDOW.

rets, the mighty central steeple whose spire rose, so tradition
tells us, to a height exceeding that of our highest existing
spire—that of St. Mary's Cathedral Church at Salisbury—
the ruined transept and the eastern arm, and all the lower
roofed domestic buildings, some of whose basement walls
would stand upon the slope of the escarpment, even as the
walls of the basement of the infirmary (if such it be) on which
the Abbey House is built still stand ; let us, further, imagine

the whole pile of buildings flushed with the rosy light of sunrise on a bright summer morning ;—and we shall have a vision of beauty such as we can in few places find in our England of the twentieth century. As the picture drawn by our imagination fades away and we see the sad reality, the mutilated remains of what was once a building of no mean order, we shall find our minds filled by conflicting emotions of regret and thankfulness—regret that so much beauty has passed away, thankfulness that so much still remains, and that it is something more than a ruin that crowns the hill before us, and that so much work of that most interesting architectural period which witnessed the development of Gothic architecture out of the Romanesque has escaped the fate that overtook so many of the religious houses of the land at the time of the dissolution of the monasteries.

G

THE WEST END.

CHAPTER III.

THE INTERIOR.

THE church is entered by the south porch, the sculpture of which has been described in the last chapter. This gives admission to that part of the south aisle which extends farther to the west than the present west end of the nave, and which has been walled up so as to form a kind of lobby. At the western end of the wall which has been built beneath the arcading that once divided the nave from the aisle may be seen a window, to the east of this a pier incorporated in the wall, then the next archway entirely blocked up. The wall that runs across the aisle to the east has been pierced by a doorway giving admission to the church, which is thus entered at the west end of the present south aisle of the building as it is now used for service. At the eastern end of the south wall of what has been called above the lobby may still be seen some traces of the arcading which once ran along the interior of the aisle walls beneath the windows. Between this and the great south doorway is a small door opening to the newel staircase by which we can reach the room over the porch and the triforium, the same staircase as that mentioned in the last chapter, to which, as there stated, admission can be obtained from the outside as well as from the inside.

When we enter the church through the door leading into the south aisle we find that a modern screen, pierced by three semicircular arches with mouldings carved in imitation of the Norman style, has been run across the church ; above this is the organ-gallery, containing a fine organ with a handsome case. The existing west end of the north aisle has been walled

83

off,[1] and now forms a kind of lumber-room, in which brooms, coal, etc., are kept.   The result of this walling-up on either

Photo.—T.P.

THE MAIN ARCADE, NORTH SIDE.

side is that within the church as it now exists we can see five bays in each aisle and six bays of the nave arcading, the

[1] This wall is the lower part of the wall that forms the easternmost of the two solid buttresses mentioned in the last chapter.

organ-gallery stretching across between the western arches on either side.

The first things that probably will catch the eyes of the visitor are the massive and somewhat short cylindrical piers of the **nave arcade**. These are perfectly plain save for the memorial tablets wherewith the bad taste of the time which succeeded the conversion of the abbey church into the parish church of the town has disfigured all the shafts, with only two exceptions. It would undoubtedly add considerably to the dignity of the arcading could these be removed; but if it were done, a chapter in the architectural history of the building would be erased, and it is by no means clear that, in some instances at any rate, the piers themselves have not been partially cut away to receive the tablets. A considerable part of the piers is hidden by the pews, with their cast-iron poppy-heads and cast scroll-work attached to the bench ends. If all these, however, were removed, and chairs used for seats, yet the bases of the pillars would still be hidden by the wooden floor, which has evidently in modern days been raised above the original level. The lowering of the floor to its original level would greatly enhance the appearance of the church.

The diameter of the cylindrical pillars is about 5 ft., the width of the arches between them about 11 ft., and their height but little exceeds two diameters; indeed, the distance from the top of the pews to the capitals is only some 7 or 8 ft. The capitals, as will be seen from the illustrations, are very simple, and are all alike with the exception of one on the south side, which bears some carving. The capitals are scalloped, and are surmounted by circular abaci. The arches of this nave arcading are pointed, but the angle is somewhat obtuse. The sectional moulding of these arches, as will be seen from the plan and illustrations, is somewhat elaborate; but with the exception of the arches in the two eastern bays, they are not ornamented with any carved work. Over every arch there was at one time a label of billet moulding, terminated by grotesque heads, the character of which will be seen on examination of the photographic illustrations. Grotesque heads of a different kind are carved at the heads of the labels. It may here be noticed that all the labels and all the heads of the arches are alike. In several cases parts of this hood moulding and one or both of its terminations have disappeared, and the whole has vanished

from above the third arch on the north side, counting from the
east.   One order of the mouldings of the two eastern arches

Photo.—T.P.

THE EASTERNMOST ARCH ON THE NORTH SIDE.

on each side is enriched by carving on the side facing the
nave.   In the eastern arches the decoration is prismatic billet,
and in the next arches star moulding.   This extra enrichment,

which may also be noticed in the string course above the arches, probably indicates the extent of the ritual choir, which, no doubt here, as elsewhere, extended one, if not two, bays westward of the crossing. The present choir screens at Westminster, Norwich, and Peterborough, are built across the structural nave, and at Christchurch, Hants, the two eastern bays of the nave triforium are much more elaborately decorated than the rest.

The string course beneath the triforium at Malmesbury is much mutilated, but it was once decorated with somewhat unusual carving, which has been imitated in the string course of the modern western screen. The **triforium** itself is very fine. The arches, decorated with chevron moulding, unlike the pointed arches below, are semicircular, thus showing that although the pointed arch had been already introduced at the time of building, the use of the round arch had not been abandoned; probably the whole was designed at the same time, though, of course, the actual masonry of the triforium must in each bay have been laid after the arch below had been completed, for there is not here any indication of the pointed arches having been a later insertion. In the eastern bay on each side the main arch of the triforium encloses three sub-arches, in the other bays four. Each of the arches rises from well-developed capitals with square abaci. The space between the mouldings surrounding the sub-arches, which are simple and uncarved, and the lowest order of the comprising arch is occupied by a plain wall. In quite recent times [1]—probably to exclude draughts—a wall has been built behind the shafts of the triforium sub-arches, which prevents any view of the church being obtained from the triforium gallery save from one spot on the south side, where under the arch of the fourth bay, counting from the east, is a curious projecting gallery, or box, which may be seen in the illustration on p. 56. Several conjectures have been made with respect to this. By some it is supposed to have been an organ-chamber, by others to have been on certain occasions the seat of the abbot. But the space seems hardly sufficient for even a small organ, and the difficulty of access renders the latter supposition improbable; it can now only be reached by crawling under or climbing over

[1] The present verger says his father remembers the building of these walls.

the massive beams that run across the space between the exterior

THE TRIFORIUM AND CLERESTORY, NORTH SIDE.

lean-to roof of the aisle and the floor over the interior vault.
But as the trusses are not the original ones, the place may have

formerly been more accessible than now. In all probability it was a **watching-chamber,** where some official passed the night to watch over the safety of the building and give notice of any sacrilegious attempt at burglary or any outbreak of fire. It is said that after the church became parochial it was used as a post of vantage from which a parish officer might note and mark the names of those present in the church at a time when absence from public worship was punishable by fines or imprisonment, though a complete view of the church could not have been obtained from this point, as those seated in the south aisle could not be seen; from what spot they were watched is not stated. But that this watching-chamber was at one time used for this purpose was stated to be a fact by Canon Jackson at a meeting of the Wilts Archæological Society, on the authority of an old man who remembered the place being so used.

What the windows of the original **clerestory** were we cannot now tell, as this part of the building was much modified in the fourteenth century. A passage runs beneath all the windows, save the two easternmost on each side, passing through the thickness of the wall between the windows. The windows now, save those in the eastern bays, which are two-light windows, have each three lights, and their tracery is of fourteenth-century character. Much of it has already been renewed, and those windows which have not as yet been touched will shortly be taken in hand. The shafts which support the roofs spring without bases from the imposts of the main piers of the nave, and the vaulting ribs spring from carved capitals formed by carrying the string course above the triforium round the vaulting shafts. The system of vaulting is thoroughly Gothic in principle, the thrust of the roof being counteracted by the external flying buttresses described in the last chapter.

The piers that once sustained the **central tower** were formed by clustered columns, and hence the easternmost arches of the nave, as we see it now, rise on their eastern sides from clustered shafts with rectangular abaci, and not from cylindrical pillars.

The east end is formed by the insertion of a plain wall beneath the original western arch of the central tower, as described in Chapter I. Against the lower part of this stands the **rood-screen,** probably removed from its original position farther west at a time when the tower was seen to be in an unsafe condition.   The screen is 11 ft. 6 in. in height, and along the top runs a cornice ornamented with a twenty-six square square paterae, carved with various devices, such as a Tudor rose, portcullis, griffins, etc.   In the centre are the arms of Henry VII., on which the English leopards are quartered with the French lilies.   The supporters are, on the right hand a dragon, and on the left some animal, possibly a

Photo.—T.P.

THE VAULT OF NAVE.

greyhound, though as the head and limbs have disappeared, it is difficult to identify.   Above the cornice runs a battlemented parapet.   The rood-screen was pierced by a central doorway; this is now, of course, walled up.   Over the cornice hangs a painting of the raising of Lazarus, said to be a copy of one painted by Michael Angelo, presented to the church by the Duke of Suffolk.

The **vault** of the nave is of stone, except that part which covers the two western bays.   Here the fall of the tower destroyed the roof, and when the church was repaired these two bays were covered with a plaster roof in imitation of the original stone vault. So close is the resemblance of the plaster to the stone that from the floor of the church the difference can hardly be detected. Mr. Prior speaks in terms of high praise of this roof, saying, "the grace and strength of the traceried vault make it one of the most vigorous examples of the fourteenth century."[1] He also speaks of the clerestory as having "lifted the Romanesque construction of 1130 another five-and-twenty feet"; but in this, even apart from the date, there is a mistake, as some part of the clerestory walls are of twelfth-century date, and their height was slightly increased by the fourteenth-century builder. A stone vault seems to have been intended from the very first, as the vaulting shafts rising from the imposts of the main piers are not fourteenth-century additions. No doubt a wooden ceiling was at first put on, but this was only a temporary contrivance, intended to give place to stone as soon as funds would allow the complete design to be executed. During the thirteenth century time and money seem to have

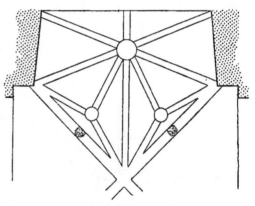

DIAGRAM OF NORTH WINDOW VAULTING.

been devoted to the enlargement of the domestic buildings, and when these were completed the abbot of the day turned his attention once more to the church, and vaulted it with stone, and made sundry other minor alterations in the fabric.

The quadripartite vaulting of the **aisles** remains as the twelfth-century builder left it (see p. 92), with the exception that in two bays on the south side and in one on the north side one quarter of the filling was cut out in the fourteenth century, when the large Decorated windows were inserted. This was an easy matter on the south side, where the heads of the windows could be kept low, the enlarged area of the windows being obtained by bringing the sills down; but on the north

[1] "History of Gothic Art in England," p. 360.

side this could not be done, owing to the south walk of the
cloister, and a gable had to be raised. This led to a com-
plicated system of vaulting ribs being used, which can best be
understood by reference to the plan on the preceding page.
The general vaulting of the aisles is of the greatest interest,
as it is a very early example of rib vaulting. It is thus

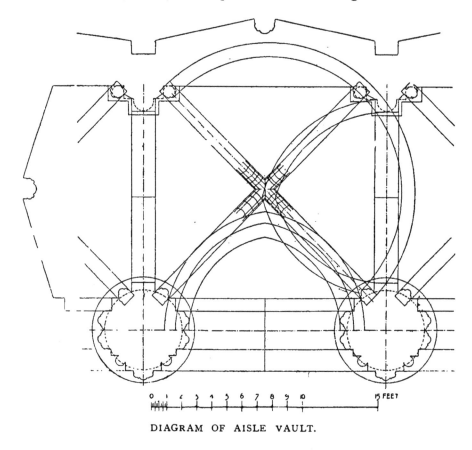

DIAGRAM OF AISLE VAULT.

described by Mr. Bilson (who has kindly allowed his plan to
be here reproduced), in a paper published in the *Journal* of
the Royal Institute of British Architects :

"The aisle vaults are supported on the one side by the
great cylindrical piers of the main arcades, and on the other
by triple shafts on the aisle wall. The arches of the main
arcades and the transverse ribs of the aisle vaults are all
pointed, the latter being of square unmoulded section. The

diagonal ribs are semicircular, and their section shows three large rolls with two smaller rolls between them. The keys of the diagonal ribs are placed higher than those of the arcade arches and transverse ribs; the surface of the vault cells at the key of the diagonal rib is 1 ft. 5 in. above the surface at the apex of the transverse arches, and 2 ft. above the surface at the apex of the arcade arches and the apex of the vault on the aisle wall."

The difference of level of the surface of the vaulting at the intersection of the diagonal ribs and at the apex of each transverse arch—a common feature in Continental vaults—is one of the arguments brought forward by Professor Moore to substantiate his assertion that the vaulting of Malmesbury aisles is an imitation of French forms, though a somewhat similar arrangement may be seen in the earlier vaulting of the choir aisles at Durham, the date of which is accurately known —namely, 1128–1133. At Malmesbury, however, the pointed arch is used more systematically than at Durham.

Along the interior of the south wall of the aisle ran an arcade consisting of three round-headed arches in each bay, springing from capitals with square abaci resting on shafts. This arcading, however, was much interfered with at various times, especially when the larger windows were inserted. Thus, for instance, on the south side in the first and second bays to the west of the wall across the aisle, the central arch of the three has been entirely cut away, and part of each of the side ones, in order to bring down the splay beneath the original window; this no doubt was an alteration made with the intention of getting more light. The same may be noticed in the fifth bay within the chapel formed by a screen; while in the third and fourth bays, where the large Decorated windows mentioned above have been inserted, the arcading has altogether disappeared, its place being occupied by added masonry, which increases the thickness of the wall. On the north side more of the arcading remains. In the first bay outside the east wall of the chamber devoted to keeping various lumber, the three arches with their shafts remain; in the next the arches and one pillar may still be seen, as also in the fourth bay; while in the fifth the easternmost arch is blocked. On this side, as mentioned in the last chapter, the sills of the windows are at a higher level than on the south, on account of the

cloister having been on this side of the church, and consequently there is room above the arcading and below the
windows for a string course with chevron ornament ; this runs
at a higher level in the fifth bay.   The east end of each aisle
is blocked' with masonry under the arch which formerly led
into the crossing.   In the north aisle, however, a doorway is
cut in the inserted wall.   The last bay of each aisle is converted into a chapel, now used for a vestry, by a screen running
north and south, and by a screen inserted beneath the main

Photo.—T.P.

WALL ARCADE, NORTH SIDE.

arcading on each side.   These screens are said by some to
have been brought to this church from the neighbouring parish
church of St. Paul, when it was finally closed, but Mr. Brakspear
says they are in situ and are the continuations of the front
screen of the " Pulpitum."

In the chapel at the end of the north aisle may be seen
a stone tablet in memory of T. Stump, and also a small
brass tablet, on which we can read the words, " Gift of
T Stump Malmesbury Abby Gent 1689."

On the east wall of the corresponding chapel on the other side are two memorial tablets; the lower one, dated 1625, bears a long and curious inscription in memory of Dame Cicely Marshall.

Deo Opt: Max:
   et   } SACRV̆.
Posteris

Stay Gentle passenger, and Read

Thy doome, I am, thow mvst be dead

In assvred Hope of a Ioyfvll resvrreccoñ heere rests deposited all ꝥ. was mortall of ꝥ Religiovs & Vertvovs Lady dame Cyscely Marshall davghter of ꝥ Hoᴸᴱ Sᴿ: Owen Hopton Kᴛ late lieftenant of ꝥ Towre royal ꝥ Faythfvll Modist & loyall wife of Sᴿ: George Marshall Kᴛ whether transcended in her more ꝥ ornamᴛˢ ꝥ beavtified A wife A mother or A matrone is still a question betwixte hir (all disconsolate) Hvsband Davghter servants, onely this is agreed vppon on all hands ꝥ svch were her perfections in each estate ꝥ in vaine will any epitaph endeavovr to delyneate them, what was her Faith Hope Charity temperanc piety patience may (to better pvrpose) be expected from ꝥ Trvmpe of an Arch Angel in ꝥ day of Gods generall retrybvcoñ, then from ꝥ faynt & flagging attrybvcons, of any particvler penn To Close all w̋ her Close, theis two spiritvall eiacvlatons, Miserere mei Devs & Domine recipe animã meam were ꝥ wings wheron ꝥ last breath ot this tvrtle movnted towards heaven to whose sweete Memory her sad Mate hath devoted this poore Monnvmᵀ· which, oh, let no prophane

HAND VIOLATE.

Emigravit 2 Apryll

Anno salvt: 1625

    Xᴿvs ⎫ ⎧ vita
    Mors ⎬ Mihi ⎨ via
    Cælv ⎭ ⎩ patria

Outside this chapel, against the screen that runs beneath the easternmost arch of the nave arcading, is the only effigy that the church contains, said by tradition to be that of **Athelstan** the Glorious, one of the great benefactors of the town and Abbey of Malmesbury. There is no inscription to identify it. The recumbent figure rests upon an altar tomb of Perpendicular character (see *ante*, p. 39).

Whether this statue was intended to represent King Athelstan or not, it was in any case not carved until many centuries after his death, and has been removed to its present position from some other spot. William of Malmesbury tells us that the king was buried at the altar of St. Mary in the tower. He also adds that he had once seen the body of the king in his coffin, and that he must in life have been of becoming stature, thin in person, and that his hair was flaxen in hue, and that it was still twined with the gold thread which he wore in his lifetime. Of course the present church was not in existence when the great West Saxon hero was laid to rest, so that the coffin may have been removed from its original grave, and it may have been in course of the removal that William of Malmesbury saw it. This monument is said to have been removed from a building on the north side of the presbytery to its present site when the eastern arm of the church became a ruin. It is also stated on the authority of a manuscript letter of Anthony Wood who visited the church in 1678, that during the civil wars the head of the statue was broken off and destroyed, and that the inhabitants put on the present head in its place ; but whether it resembled the former one or not he could not say. The head of the lion on which the feet rest is also a reproduction. Several authorities, among them John Britton, assert that this monument has no reference to Althelstan ; but it is by no means unlikely that tradition is here correct, and that this statue was intended to keep alive in the town which he so much benefited, and which he chose as the burying-place of two nephews and himself, the name and fame of the victor of Brunanburh.

From what has been already said, it will be understood that the church as it now stands has no chancel, and it is not likely that any attempt to build one will be made. The communion table stands against the east wall, and the altar rails project, in the form of three sides of a rectangle, in front and at either end of it. A little distance in front of the rails on the south side stands the pulpit, and on the north the reading-desk. As we stand in front of the rails we shall notice how on each side the capitals of the easternmost cylindrical pillar have been mutilated, apparently with the intention of inserting some

THE FONT.

wooden beam. In fact, it is said that at one time not only the cloister, chapels, and domestic buildings were used as weavers' workshops, but that looms were even introduced into the nave itself.

The **font** stands near the western screen.

The general effect of the church is not so imposing as it

would be if it were longer ; the blank wall at the east end still further detracts from its appearance. To run out a chancel would no doubt be a suggestion that would meet with much favour, but it would be wholly unjustifiable, as it could not well be done without interfering with the fine ruined tower arch to the north-east of the church, and would also interfere with the old rood-loft now incorporated in the eastern wall. More length would be gained if the modern organ-gallery were swept away and the organ placed—as suggested in the joint report of the Society of Antiquaries and the Society for the Protection of Ancient Buildings—over the altar. In this position it would help to break the plain expanse of the eastern wall, and would be near the choir, if seats were arranged for the choristers at the east end of the church. The rebuilding of the ruined part at the west end in the manner indicated in Chapter I. would also give extra length to the church. The pews might well be swept away and the floor lowered so as to show the bases of the pillars. One other alteration should be made ; the gas-jets are now placed so close to the triforium walls that the heat and fumes are likely to lead to the decay of the stone ; it would be far better if electric-lighting could be used, but if this cannot be introduced, the gas standards or pendants should be kept well away from the walls.

CHAPTER IV.

THE ABBOTS OF MALMESBURY.

A COMPLETE list of the abbots is not in existence, but such as are known will be mentioned.

EALDHELM was the first real abbot, though Maldulf had preceded him in charge of the religious community existing at Malmesbury, which, however, had not been formally created an abbey until about the year 680, when Eleutherius appointed Ealdhelm. In 705 he was consecrated Bishop of Sherborne. According to some authorities, DANIEL succeeded either at the time of his appointment as bishop or on his death in 709. William of Malmesbury makes no mention of Daniel, but speaks of a second Ealdhelm, nephew of the saint, as the next abbot. ÆTHELHEARD was the next abbot, and resigned his office on being consecrated Bishop of Winchester in 780. To him succeeded CUTHBERT, who died about 796.

A gap here occurs of nearly 200 years. Abbots, of course, there were, but their names have been lost. It may be that the records were destroyed when King Edwy expelled the monks for a time. The first of the new series of abbots was ÆLFRIC, appointed by Edgar about 974. He became Bishop of Crediton in 977, and was succeeded at Malmesbury by ÆTHELWERD; his successors were KINEWERD, BRIHTHELM BRIHTWOLD I., EADRIC, WULSINE, EGELWARD, EALWINE, BRIHTWOLD II.—the abbot whose body was exhumed and cast into a marsh. Herman, Bishop of Sarum, during the vacancy claimed the abbey; but the monks obtained the support of Earl Godwine, and elected BRITHRIC. He was deposed by William the Conqueror, who placed TURALD, a monk of Fechamp in Normandy, over the abbey. He became Abbot of

Peterborough in 1070, and WARIN DE LYRÂ became abbot in 1070. GODFREY DE JUMIEGE, who came from Ely, succeeded him in 1081. It is recorded that he wore a brazen ring around his body; he was a great collector of books for the abbey library. EDULF, a monk from Winchester, succeeded him in 1106, and ruled the abbey till Bishop Roger of Sarum deposed him in 1118 and constituted himself head of the abbey till his death. JOHN became Abbot in 1140, and held the office for a few months only. During this time an attack was made on the abbey by one Robert, who came from the castle at Devizes, and slew all the monks who had not sought safety in flight. PETER was chosen abbot in 1141. He was succeeded by GREGORY about 1159, and Gregory by ROBERT about 1174. OSBERT, Prior of Gloucester, became abbot in 1180, and died in 1181 or 1182. NICHOLAS, a monk of St. Albans and then Prior of Wallingford, was the next abbot. He was deposed in 1187, and RORERT DE MELUN, sub-Prior of Winchester, took his place. He died about 1208, and WALTER DE LORING succeeded to his office. On his death in 1222 JOHN, a Welshman, became abbot. His name is found among those who signed the deed executed in 1222 confirming the Great Charter originally granted by King John. GEOFFREY was abbot from 1246 to 1260. WILLIAM DE COLERNE, who has already been mentioned in Chapter I. as a great builder of the domestic offices of the abbey, became abbot in 1260, and held the post till his death. WILLIAM DE BADMINTON became abbot in 1296. ADAM DE LA HOOKE, who refused a place of burial within the walls of his church to the body of Edward II., succeeded him in 1324. In the records of Edward III. there is a grant of a pardon to the Abbot of Malmesbury who was charged with giving shelter to one of the murderers of Edward II., but whether the shelter was given at the time of the murder by Adam or later by his successor is not very clear. If Adam were the guilty party, it may be that his refusal to grant a grave to Edward II. was due to a feeling of hostility towards him.

Of the remaining abbots a list with the dates of their entering on their office will suffice, for we know little of them beyond their names: JOHN DE TINTERN, 1339; SIMON DU AUMENEY, 1348; WALTER CAMME,[1] 1360; THOMAS DE

---

[1] He was the first mitred abbot.

CHELESWORTH, 1395; ROBERT PERSHORE, 1424; THOMAS BRISTOWE, 1434; JOHN ANDOVER, 1456; JOHN AYLEE, 1462; THOMAS OLVESTON, 1480; ROBERT FRAMPTON, or SELWYN, 1533. He was the last abbot, and surrendered the abbey to Henry VIII. on December 15, 1539.

The last abbot received a pension of £133 6s. 8d., the other twenty-one pensioners sums varying from £13 16s. 8d. to £6. In the year 1553 the Pension Rolls mention only seven recipients of the pensions; the ex-abbot and the others were by this time dead. Of those living in 1553, WALTER STACEY, formerly steward of the abbey lands, RICHARD ASHETON, marked in 1533 as farmer, and two priests, THOMAS FROSTER and THOMAS STANLEY, are marked as married. Evidently they had taken advantage of the dissolution of their monastery and the growing Protestantism of the age to disregard their former vows.

Malmesbury Abbey is now a vicarage in the gift of the trustees of the late Rev. C. Kemble, and, though in the county of Wilts, is in the Diocese of Bristol. The town is reached by a branch line of the Great Western Railway running from Dauntsey station. Dauntsey is 87½ miles from Paddington, and the branch line is 6½ miles in length. A new loop of the Great Western Railway is now being made from Wootton-Basset to the Severn Tunnel to shorten the distance from London to South Wales. This will pass not far south of Malmesbury, and should a station be made where the new line crosses the branch from Dauntsey, it will somewhat shorten the distance.

THE CHURCH OF ST. LAURENCE
AT BRADFORD-ON-AVON.

Photo.—T.P.

THE CHURCHES OF BRADFORD-ON-AVON FROM THE NORTH-EAST.

THE CHURCH OF ST. LAURENCE
AT BRADFORD-ON-AVON.

THE little Church of St. Laurence, at Bradford-on-Avon, easily reached by the Great Western Railway either from Bath or Malmesbury, is in its foundation closely connected with the abbey at the latter place, and is one of the most interesting buildings in the country. We have many fragments of churches in various parts of England, some undoubtedly of earlier date than this church at the Wiltshire Bradford; but this is the earliest complete church of which we have documentary evidence, fixing its date within the limits of a few years. Owing to its peculiar history, the building as we see it now differs little in form and dimensions from what it was when first erected. It must not, however, be supposed that all its walls have stood intact from the time of its first erection, about the year 700, to the present day. Some of the stones which we now see in the walls were at some unknown period displaced, converted to other uses, or even buried beneath the soil which accumulated round the building; but they have been discovered and put back into their former positions, and some new stones have of necessity been added. Unfortunately those responsible for the restoration decorated in some places this new stone-work with certain ornamental features to make it match the old, instead of leaving it perfectly plain, so as to mark the difference between the original and the modern work; indeed, to the writer it seems as if in such a case as this it would have been better to use some different material, such as brick, for the repairs, so that no one could, in any future ages, fail to distinguish the work of the nineteenth-century restorer from that of the old Wessex builder.

William of Malmesbury speaks of a church as standing at Bradford in his own day, which he says was built by St. Ealdhelm, the founder of the abbey at Malmesbury. His words are: "Et est ad hunc diem eo loci Ecclesiola quam ad nomen beatissimi Laurentii fecisse predicatur Aldhelmus" ("De Gestis Pontificum"). From this we learn that a church existed at Bradford in the early part of the twelfth century, which had been built by the Abbot of Malmesbury at any rate before 705, when he became Bishop of Sherborne, for a deed at the time of his consecration mentions the monasteries which he had founded at Frome and Bradford. By the word "monastery" we must not understand a large establishment with church, cloister, refectory, dormitory, bakery, brewery, mill, and all the other adjuncts to a monastery, whether Benedictine or Cistercian, of the twelfth or thirteenth century, but a kind of mission-station where two or three priests resided and ministered to the spiritual wants of the district. The only necessary buildings would be a church and a small attached dwelling-house. Bradford, as well as Malmesbury, was comprised within the limits of the See of Sherborne, and both looked up to their founder, Bishop Ealdhelm, as their head.

No notice of anything connected with this church occurs for nearly three hundred years after Ealdhelm's death; but in 1001 we find that King Æthelred II. bestowed the monastery (*coenobium*) with the adjacent manor (*cum undique adjacente . villâ*) on the Abbess of Shaftesbury, in order to provide the nuns with a safe retreat (*impenetrabile confugium*), in case they were attacked at Shaftesbury by the Danes, and also in order that they might be able to hide there the precious relics of King Edward, murdered, at the instigation of his stepmother, as he left the gateway of her abode, which once stood somewhere near the site of that Corfe Castle whose ruins we see to-day. His body, found at a spot near Wareham, to which his horse had dragged it, was first buried at Wareham and afterwards carried to Shaftesbury. Æthelred directed that when peace should be restored to his kingdom, the nuns should return to Shaftesbury, though some of them might, if they preferred it—but only with full consent of the abbess—remain at Bradford. We may perhaps

wonder why the nuns should be safer at Bradford than at
Shaftesbury, but the reason is not far to seek : Shaftesbury is
built upon a lofty hill some 700 ft. above the sea level, and the
abbey stood on the highest part of the hill, and must have
been a conspicuous object for many miles round ; whereas,
Bradford lies in a hollow, and was surrounded on all sides by
woods, which would make it a spot difficult of access for a
body of troops. Thus from the year 1001 until the days of
Henry VIII., when Shaftesbury Abbey, like all the other
monasteries and nunneries, was dissolved, the church at
Bradford remained in the hands of the powerful and wealthy
Abbess of Shaftesbury.

The Manor of Bradford then passed into lay hands, and
with it went the little church of St. Ealdhelm's building,
and its character as a church was soon forgotten. In
1715 it was in the hands of one Anthony Methuen, who, as
lessee, with the consent of the lord of the manor, granted
part of the building—that is to say, what had been the
nave and porch—to the Rev. John Roger, Vicar of Bradford,
for use as a parish school. The chancel did not go with
the rest. The chancel arch was destroyed and a wall built to
entirely separate it from the nave ; whether this was done in
1715 or had been done previously, we do not know.· The
deed of gift speaks of it as a " building adjoining the churchyard in Bradford, commonly called or known by the name of
the Skull house," from which it would appear that it had at
some time been used as a charnel-house. The chancel was
used as a cottage. . In course of time other buildings rose
round it, and it was completely forgotten ; no one dreamed of
its being the Church of St. Laurence. In 1856, however, the
Rev. W. B. Jones, Vicar of Bradford, was asked to read a paper
at the meeting of the Wilts Archæological Society, which had
been arranged for the following year, on the antiquities of
Bradford ; and here it may be incidentally mentioned that even
apart from this little church there is much of antiquarian
interest in the town, among other things the chapel on the
bridge over the Avon. Mr. Jones climbed to the top of a
hill on the north side of the town, on which stood the ruins
of St. Mary's Chapel, in order to survey the remains at that
place ; and then, as he looked down on the town which lay
outspread below him, his eye caught sight of three ridges of

roof slightly higher than the surrounding buildings which seemed to him to indicate the outline of nave, chancel, and porch of some old church. He brought his conjectures to the notice of the meeting, but his idea that these buildings were the remains of some forgotten church did not meet with

Photo.—T.P.

THE WEST END AND NORTH PORCH.

much favour from those present. Professor Freeman, Sir Gilbert Scott, and Mr. Petit were convinced that the building was of great age, but the general opinion was that the masonry was far too good for the end of the seventh century. The walls are fine jointed ; and as it was then a generally accepted article of belief that no fine-jointed masonry of earlier date than the twelfth century was to be found, it was assumed that this building could not have an earlier date. This view

Photo.—T.P.

THE EAST WALL OF THE NAVE.

was combated in an article in *The Saturday Review* for October 19th, 1872 (probably written by Professor E. A. Freeman). In it the writer said that Beda's account of the rough stone-work of northern churches of early date did not necessarily imply that finer work might not be found in the south, especially at a spot where the common building-stone was the Bath oolite, so easily worked to smooth faces. From this time forward the opinion that this building was St. Ealdhelm's work gradually gained ground.

In 1872 the chancel was purchased, and after some difficulty with the Charity Commissioners, who insisted on the preservation of the interests of the Endowed School, the rest of the building was handed over by the trustees of the charity to the purchasers of the chancel in exchange for the old Church House, built, as Leland informs us, in the fifteenth century.

The restoration of the building then commenced, and it now stands with an open space round it, all the other buildings that once blocked it in having been cleared away. In removing sundry chimney-stacks and digging up the floors many of the original stones were discovered, and these were put back into their former places.

The church, as it now stands, consists of a nave 25 ft. 2 in. by 13 ft. 2 in., a north porch 10 ft. 5 in. by 9 ft. 11 in., and a chancel 13 ft. 2 in. by 10 ft. Two features are very noticeable : first, the great height in proportion to the width and length of the building ; and, secondly, the small size and number of the windows. The side walls of the nave are 25 ft. 5 in. in height, those of the chancel 18 ft. 4 in., and those of the porch 15 ft. 6 in. There are only three narrow windows in the building—one in the nave, another in the chancel (both on the south side), and a third on the west side of the porch. Great height in proportion to length seems to have been a usual feature in so-called Saxon churches. We meet with it at Deerhurst, at Wareham, and at Escomb, in the county of Durham[1]; and it is possible that these buildings may have been divided into two stories. On the north wall of St. Laurence's are some marks of effaced brackets or rafter holes on a level with the top of the chancel arch ; these, however, may have been inserted at the time when the building was arranged for domestic purposes.

---

[1] Early drawings of churches often represent these as short and high. It was once thought that these were mere conventional representations, but in all probability they indicated pretty accurately the proportions that formerly prevailed.

The walls of the nave and the east wall of the chancel are divided on the outside into three stages. The lowest is quite plain with the exception of some shallow pilasters, formed by cutting away the rest of the wall and leaving them slightly projecting. The lower stage is divided from that above it by a string course which runs at the same level all round the building. The second stage is ornamented with arcading formed of semicircular-headed arches, rising from a row of flat pilasters with bases and capitals. This arcade is simply ornamental, the whole being formed by cutting away the stone and leaving the pilasters and arches projecting, not by constructing arches in the usual way. The stone is laid in regular courses without any reference to the arches. It would seem that this stage was originally built quite plain, and when the walls were finished the decoration was added by cutting into the surface. In some cases the arches are only cut out below, in other cases both below and above. In the porch there are no arches in the second stage, simply

Photo.—T.P.

DOORWAY IN NORTH PORCH.

pilasters running up to the table below the eaves. The arcade in the chancel wall is more elaborately cut than in the nave. In the gable of the eastern wall of the chancel are remains of several moulded pilasters, the arches above them being more and more stilted towards the centre.

The church is entered by a PORCH on the north side. On its front in the gable it had a series of moulded pilasters, most of one of which and smaller parts of two others still remain.

Beneath these is a string course level with the eaves; below this a stage ornamented with pilasters, and in the lower stage the doorway. The head of the doorway is semicircular, but

THE CHANCEL ARCH.

stilted, springing from imposts, and is surrounded by a hood moulding also resting on imposts. The north face of the porch is not quite parallel to the wall of the church, its eastern side being a few inches longer than the western. The doorway is not in the centre of the north wall of the porch, but much nearer to the western wall. Like the other openings in this church, it is exceedingly narrow. The doorway from the porch into the church is placed centrally, and is rather wider—2 ft. 10 in.—and is 8 ft. 6 in. high, measuring from the floor to the centre of the arch. The side walls of the doorway incline so that the opening is a little narrower at the springing of the arch than at the floor. On the left-hand side is a moulded pilaster of three flattened roundels supporting a plain impost and a projecting hood moulding. Towards the eastern end of the south side of the nave there is a window. Only a few fragments of the original window remain, but these sufficed for a conjectural restoration. Windows had been inserted in the west wall to give light to the building when used as a school, interfering with the external arcading ; this, however, has been restored.

From the nave we pass into the chancel through an extremely narrow arch measuring 3 ft. 5 in. in width, while the height is about 10 ft. The sides converge towards the top. On the west face it has a hood moulding of three bands (which are tolerably perfect on the south side) and imposts extending into

Photo.—T.P.

VIEW FROM THE CHANCEL.

the walls. There are incisions in the arch just below the impost, into which probably were driven wooden blocks; in these the staples were inserted on which the chancel gates hung. High above the chancel arch, on the western face, are two carved figures of angels in low relief, their heads surrounded by aureoles, their wings extended, and with maniples hanging over their arms.   The stones on which they are carved are shaped as if intended to form the angles of a classical pediment, and may have been part of a reredos of an altar placed in the upper story, if the supposition that the

CARVED ANGELS ON THE EAST WALL OF THE NAVE.

church was so divided is correct.   The present position of these figures is the same as that in which they were discovered at the time of the restoration.

The chancel window, situated a little to the east of the middle of the south side, is about 3 ft. 6 in. in height, round-headed, and considerably splayed both inside and out.   The sides converge slightly. The floor of the chancel is somewhat lower than that of the nave.

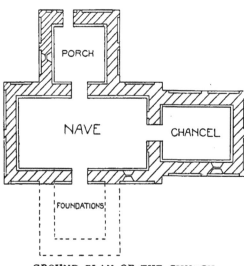

GROUND PLAN OF THE CHURCH.

On the south side, op-posite to the north porch, and giving the building a cruciform plan, was a building, possibly the residence of the priest or priests.   At the time of the discovery of the church a cottage occupied this site.   Part of the eastern wall of this was the original wall.   The marks of the gable of this building, after the removal of plaster, might be seen beneath the roof of the cottage on the south wall, and also marks showing where the original west wall of this southward projection abutted against the wall of the church. The arcading which surrounds the building terminated where the two side walls met the south wall of the church. This cottage has been entirely cleared away, and two large buttresses have been built with

THE SOUTH SIDE.

their bases on the foundations of the east and west walls of the original southern projection. A doorway gave entrance from this to the nave, but was of a much plainer character than the door on the north side.

DIMENSIONS OF BATH ABBEY.

Length : Interior, along aisles	212 ft.
Width of nave and choir	72 ,,
Length of nave, interior	106 ,,
,, ,, choir ,,	67 ,,
,, ,, transept ,,	122 ,,
Width of transept	20 ,,
,, ,, tower, east to west, exterior	28 ,,
,, ,, ,, north to south, exterior	40 ,,
Height of vault	75 ,,
,, ,, tower	162 ,,
Area	16,600 sq. feet.

DIMENSIONS OF MALMESBURY ABBEY.

EXISTING PART.

Length : Exterior, south aisle, including ruined part	160 ft.
,, Interior, south aisle, as now used	81 ,,
,, ,, of nave of existing church	94 ,,
,, ,, ,, north aisle	97 ,,
Width : Exterior of nave and aisles	84 ,,
,, Interior of nave	33 ,,
,, ,, ,, aisles	13 ,,
Thickness of aisle walls	8 ,,
Height of nave vault	about 65 ,,
Area	about 9,500 feet.

PORCH.

Width, east to west, exterior, exclusive of buttresses	33 ,,
Length, west to south	24 ,,

RUINOUS OR NON-EXISTENT.

Sides of central tower (interior)	30 ,,
Length of transept (exterior)	166 ,,
Total length of building	about 300 ,,
Length of lady-chapel	about 60 ,,
Width of lady-chapel	15 ,,

CHISWICK PRESS : PRINTED BY CHARLES WHITTINGHAM AND CO.
TOOKS COURT, CHANCERY LANE, LONDON.

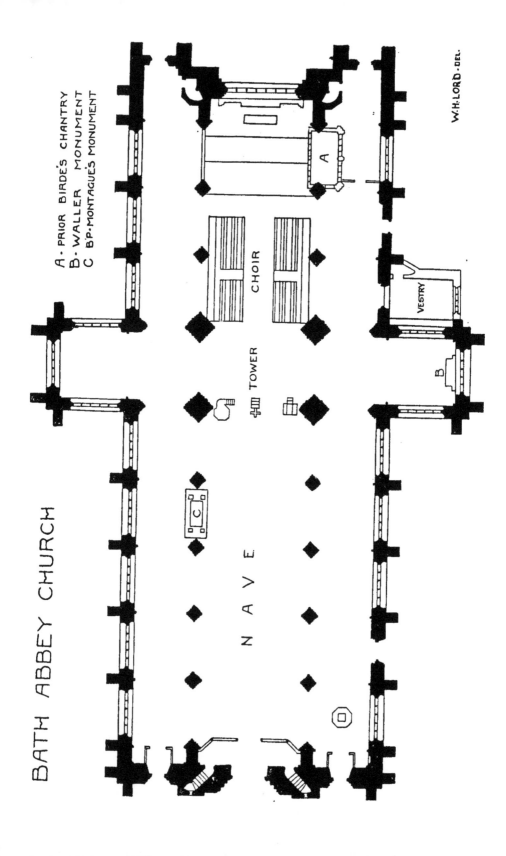

BATH ABBEY CHURCH

A · PRIOR BIRDE'S CHANTRY
B · WALLER MONUMENT
C · BP · MONTAGUE'S MONUMENT

A

CHOIR

VESTRY

B

TOWER

C

N A V E

W·H·LORD·DEL·

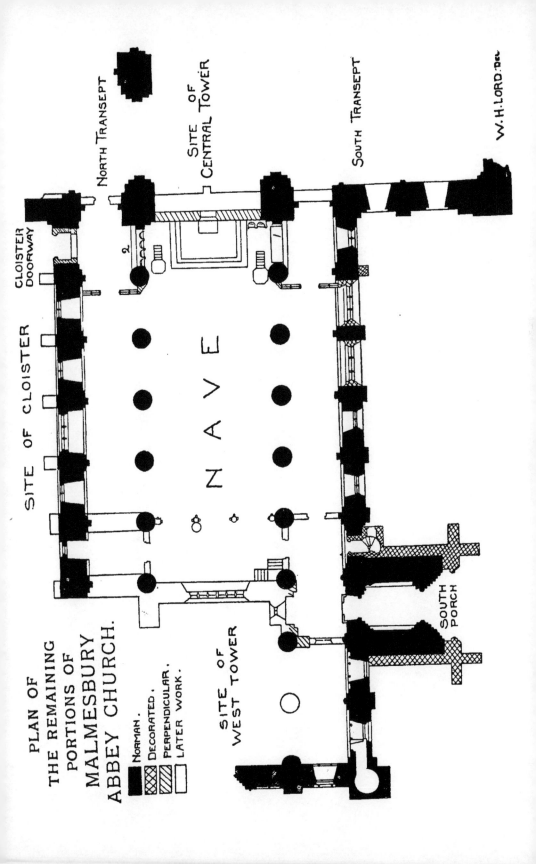

PLAN OF
THE REMAINING
PORTIONS OF
MALMESBURY
ABBEY CHURCH.

NORMAN.
DECORATED.
PERPENDICULAR.
LATER WORK.

SITE OF CLOISTER

CLOISTER
DOORWAY

NORTH TRANSEPT

SITE
OF
CENTRAL TOWER

NAVE

SOUTH TRANSEPT

SITE OF
WEST TOWER

SOUTH
PORCH

W. H. LORD. DEL.

Bell's Cathedral Series.

Profusely Illustrated.   Cloth, crown 8vo, **1s. 6d.** *net each.*

NOW READY.

ENGLISH CATHEDRALS. An Itinerary and Description. Compiled by JAMES G. GILCHRIST, A.M., M.D. Revised and edited with an Introduction on Cathedral Architecture by the Rev. T. PERKINS, M.A., F.R.A.S.

BRISTOL. By H. J. L. J. MASSÉ, M.A.

CANTERBURY. By HARTLEY WITHERS   3rd Edition, revised.

CARLISLE. By C. K. ELEY.

CHESTER. By CHARLES HIATT. 2nd Edition, revised.

DURHAM. By J. E. BYGATE, A.R.C.A. 2nd Edition.

ELY. By Rev. W. D. SWEETING, M.A.

EXETER. By PERCY ADDLESHAW, B.A. 2nd Edition.

GLOUCESTER. By H. J. L. J. MASSÉ, M.A. 2nd Edition.

HEREFORD. By A. HUGH FISHER, A.R.E. 2nd Edition, revised.

LICHFIELD. By A. B. CLIFTON. 2nd Edition, revised.

LINCOLN. By A. F. KENDRICK, B.A. 2nd Edition, revised.

NORWICH. By C. H. B. QUENNELL. 2nd Edition.

OXFORD. By Rev. PERCY DEARMER, M.A. 2nd Edition, revised.

PETERBOROUGH. By Rev. W. D. SWEETING, M.A. 2nd Edition.

RIPON. By CECIL HALLET, B.A.

ROCHESTER. By G. H. PALMER, B.A. 2nd Edition.

ST. DAVID'S. By PHILIP ROBSON, A.R.I.B.A.

ST. PAUL'S. By Rev. ARTHUR DIMOCK, M.A. 2nd Edition.

SALISBURY. By GLEESON WHITE. 2nd Edition, revised.

SOUTHWELL. By Rev. ARTHUR DIMOCK, M.A. 2nd Edition, revised.

WELLS. By Rev. PERCY DEARMER, M.A. 2nd Edition, revised.

WINCHESTER. By P. W. SERGEANT. 2nd Edition, revised.

WORCESTER. By EDWARD F. STRANGE.

YORK. By A. CLUTTON BROCK. 2nd Edition, revised.

Preparing.

CHICHESTER. By H. C. CORLETTE, A.R.I.B.A.

ST. ALBANS. By Rev. W. D. SWEETING, M.A.

ST. ASAPH'S and BANGOR. By P. B. IRONSIDE BAX.

GLASGOW. By P. MACGREGOR CHALMERS, I.A., F.S.A. (Scot).

LLANDAFF. By HERBERT PRIOR.

Uniform with above Series. **1s. 6d.** *net each.*

ST. MARTIN'S CHURCH, CANTERBURY. By Rev. CANON ROUTLEDGE, M.A., F.S.A. 24 Illustrations.

BEVERLEY MINSTER. By CHARLES HIATT. 47 Illustrations.

WIMBORNE MINSTER AND CHRISTCHURCH PRIORY. By Rev. T. PERKINS, M.A., F.R.A.S. 65 Illustrations.

TEWKESBURY ABBEY AND DEERHURST PRIORY. By H. J. L. J. MASSÉ, M.A. 44 Illustrations.

BATH ABBEY, MALMESBURY ABBEY, AND BRADFORD-ON-AVON CHURCH. By Rev. T. PERKINS, M.A.

WESTMINSTER ABBEY. By CHARLES HIATT.   *[Preparing.*

Bell's Handbooks to Continental Churches.

Profusely Illustrated.   Crown 8vo, cloth, **2s. 6d.** *net each.*

CHARTRES: The Cathedral and Other Churches.   By H. J. L. J.
MASSÉ

"For the purpose at which they aim they are admirably done, and there are few visitants to any of our noble shrines who will not enjoy their visit the better for being furnished with one of these delightful books, which can be slipped into the pocket and carried with ease, and is yet distinct and legible. . . . A volume such as that on Canterbury is exactly what we want, and on our next visit we hope to have it with us. It is thoroughly helpful, and the views of the fair city and its noble cathedral are beautiful. Both volumes, moreover, will serve more than a temporary purpose, and are trustworthy as well as delightful."—*Notes and Queries*.

"We have so frequently in these columns urged the want of cheap, well-illustrated, and well-written handbooks to our cathedrals, to take the place of the out-of-date publications of local booksellers, that we are glad to hear that they have been taken in hand by Messrs George Bell & Sons."—*St. James's Gazette*.

"The volumes are handy in size, moderate in price, well illustrated, and written in a scholarly spirit. The history of cathedral and city is intelligently set forth and accompanied by a descriptive survey of the building in all its detail. The illustrations are copious and well selected, and the series bids fair to become an indispensable companion to the cathedral tourist in England."—*Times*.

"They are nicely produced in good type, on good paper, and contain numerous illustrations, are well written, and very cheap. We should imagine architects and students of architecture will be sure to buy the series as they appear, for they contain in brief much valuable information."—*British Architect*.

"Bell's 'Cathedral Series,' so admirably edited, is more than a description of the various English cathedrals. It will be a valuable historical record, and a work of much service also to the architect. The illustrations are well selected, and in many cases not mere bald architectural drawings but reproductions of exquisite stone fancies, touched in their treatment by fancy and guided by art."—*Star*.

"Each of them contains exactly that amount of information which the intelligent visitor, who is not a specialist, will wish to have. The disposition of the various parts is judiciously proportioned, and the style is very readable. The illustrations supply a further important feature; they are both numerous and good. A series which cannot fail to be welcomed by all who are interested in the ecclesiastical buildings of England."—*Glasgow Herald*.

"Those who, either for purposes of professional study or for a cultured recreation, find it expedient to 'do' the English cathedrals will welcome the beginning of Bell's 'Cathedral Series.' This set of books is an attempt to consult, more closely, and in greater detail than the usual guide-books do, the needs of visitors to the cathedral towns. The series cannot but prove markedly successful. In each book a business-like description is given of the fabric of the church to which the volume relates, and an interesting history of the relative diocese. The books are plentifully illustrated, and are thus made attractive as well as instructive. They cannot but prove welcome to all classes of readers interested either in English Church history or in ecclesiastical architecture."—*Scotsman*.

"They have nothing in common with the almost invariably wretched local guides save portability, and their only competitors in the quality and quantity of their contents are very expensive and mostly rare works, each of a size that suggests a packing-case rather than a coat-pocket. The 'Cathedral Series' are important compilations concerning history, architecture, and biography, and quite popular enough for such as take any sincere interest in their subjects."—*Sketch*.

LONDON: GEORGE BELL AND SONS

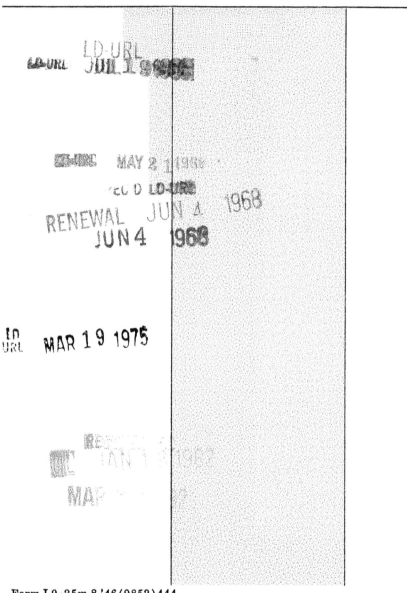

Lightning Source UK Ltd.
Milton Keynes UK
UKHW011944021218
333216UK00013B/2077/P